**DATE DUE**

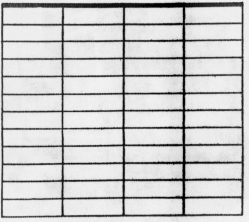

DEMCO

# CLASSIC DINERS
## OF THE NORTHEAST

(originally titled *Diners of the Northeast*)

From Maine to New Jersey,
visits to the best of the old-fashioned eateries that
made road food famous

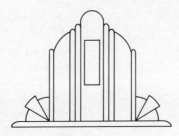

BY DONALD KAPLAN AND ALAN BELLINK
PHOTOGRAPHS BY JOHN BEAN

FABER AND FABER                                                                    BOSTON AND LONDON

## Dedication ═══════════

*To Charles P. Gemme,*
*the guiding light of the Worcester Lunch Car Company,*
*whose beautiful diners gave us so much pleasure*

*Designed by Abigail Moseley*

**Library of Congress Cataloging-in-Publication Data**

Kaplan, Donald, 1948–
    Classic diners of the Northeast.

    Rev. ed. of: Diners of the Northeast, from Maine to
New Jersey. 1st ed. c1980.
    1. Restaurants, lunch rooms, etc.—Northeastern States—
Directories.    2. Diners (Restaurants)—Northeastern
States—Directories.    I. Bellink, Alan.    II. Kaplan,
Donald, 1948–    . Diners of the Northeast, from Maine
to New Jersey.    III. Title.
TX907.K36    1986        647'.4674        86-18902
ISBN 0-571-12950-1 (pbk.)

## Contents ========================================= 5

Acknowledgments 7
Introduction 9

**Connecticut 17** ==============================
| | |
|---|---|
| Canaan | Collin's Diner 18 |
| East Hartford | Mark Twain Diner 20 |
| Fairfield | Larry's Diner 22 |
| Groton | Norms Diner 24 |
| Middletown | O'Rourke's Diner 26 |
| New Haven | Hi-Way Diner 28 |
| Newington | Olympia Diner 30 |
| Stamford | Curley's Diner 33 |
| Torrington | Skee's Diner 37 |
| Wethersfield | Makris Diner 39 |

**Maine 41** ==============================
| | |
|---|---|
| Belgrade Lakes | Old MacDonald's 42 |
| Gardiner | Wakefield's Diner 43 |
| Kittery | Seagull Diner 45 |
| Portland | Miss Portland Diner 47 |

**Massachusetts 49** ==============================
| | |
|---|---|
| Dedham | Apple Tree Diner 50 |
| Dracut | Old Colony Diner 52 |
| Florence | Miss Florence Diner 54 |
| Lowell | Owl Diner 55 |
| Natick | Casey's Diner 57 |
| New Bedford | Orchid Diner 60 |
| Palmer | Day And Night Diner 62 |
| Peabody | Red Rambler Diner 64 |

6   Pittsfield             Adrienne's Diner  65
Rowley               Agawam Diner  67
Salem                Boyle's Elm Tree Diner  68
                         Salem Diner  70
Worcester           Boulevard Diner  72
                         Miss Worcester  75

**New Hampshire  77**
Dover                Stoney's Diner  78
Laconia             Paugus Diner  79
Littleton            Littleton Diner  80
Portsmouth        Gilly's Lunch Wagon  83
West Lebanon      Four Aces Diner  85

**New Jersey  87**
Belmar              Pat's Riverview Diner  88
Bloomfield         Short Stop Diner  89
Burlington         Burlington Diner  91
Closter             Big "E" Diner  95
Dumont           Crystal Diner  96
Hackensack       White Manna Diner  98
Little Ferry       Rosie's Farmland Diner  101
Princeton        College Inn  104
South River       Bosko's Diner  105
Williamstown     Williamstown Diner  108
Windsor            Irene's Windsor Diner  109

**New York  113**
Astoria, Queens    Airline Diner  114
Binghamton       Danny's Diner  115
Brooklyn         Blue Bird Diner  116
Center Moriches    Duffy's Diner  117

Colonie            Charlie's Northway Diner  118
Harrison           Chinatown Diner  119
Katonah          Blue Dolphin Diner  121
Kingston          Colonial Diner  123
Lake George     Prospect Mountain Diner  125
Merrick           Marybill Diner  126
Monticello        Pioneer Diner  128
New York         Empire Diner  129
                        River Diner  130
                        Square Diner  132
North Syracuse    Mario's Diner  134
Polksville         Suburban Skyliner  135
Schenectady      Ruby's Silver Diner  136
West Taghkanic    West Taghkanic Diner  137

**Rhode Island  39**
Middletown      Tommy's Deluxe Diner  140
Providence       Ever-Ready Diner  143
                        Haven Brothers  145
                        Silvertop Diner  147
Woonsocket      Champ's Diner  149

**Vermont  151**
Bennington      Blue Benn Diner  152
Burlington       Parkway Diner  154
Chester          Delaney's Country Girl Diner  155
Newport         Miss Newport Diner  157
Rutland          Midway Diner  159

**Counter Talk  160**
Counter Talk  160

This publication is a reprint of a 1980 book originally entitled *Diners of the Northeast*. Many places described within these pages may be renovated beyond recognition as a classic diner, moved down the street, or just plain gone out of business. The passage of time has also made certain factual information out of date as well: Prices have generally risen, some diners have new owners, and neighborhoods have changed. But change is part of the adventure we have every time we take to the road, looking for the classic American diners we love.

Alan Bellink
Donald Kaplan

There are many people who contributed to this project. Unfortunately, the list is too long to thank them all by name. However, special thanks are due to: Lynn Lobban, whose energy and organizational skills helped make the photos as good as they are; Kathy Hourrigan, who helped us get through the door; Betty Thompsen, whose keen mind and passion for diners was a constant inspiration; Les Davis, for his spiritual guidance; Lecie Piggott, for her support and understanding; and Alan Gray for being there. Also, in their own special way: Helen and Norman Belink, Eleanor Kaplan, Izzy Snow, Susan Belling, Martha Kaplan, Lyda Pola, Tom Negron, Jeff Thompsen, Bob Rancan, Paul and Jane Freedman, Kenny Silverbush, Paul Wasserman, Steve Sink, Steve Mantin, and Howard King. And of course, our editor, Hugh Rawson, whose guidance and input carried us through to publication; his able assistant, Paul Heacock, who edited our sometimes garbled thoughts with the skill and grace of a veteran grillman; and, Gai Moseley, whose creativity is in evidence on every page. Finally, Norman Simpson who brought this book back to life, and Paul Fargis who introduced us to him.

As the quest for the perfect diner is all-consuming, we would like to thank all our friends who stood by us and tolerated our lengthy monologues on the ultimate plate of home fries and the perfect cup of coffee.

## *Authors Preface to the 2nd Edition*

Hold it! when we wrote this book in 1979, that cozy stainless steel diner Dad used to take you to after Sunday School was going the way of the dinosaur—toward extinction. A few places remained and "Diners of the Northeast" was our tribute to these unique American eateries which nurtured us after school, and later, after work. Unfortunately, 1979 America was bolting down fast-food hamburgers and cement-like thick shakes while whizzing down the interstate, and forsaking those cute little shiny diners where a cup of java and a "slice of apple" could be bought with loose change in your pocket, and friendly talk was just a stool away.

Then something happened. A number of movies appeared using diners as central locations and as metaphors for the adolescent dreams of the carefree '50s. The rest of the electronic and print media caught on, reminding us that many cherished moments were spent in these places of our youths with families, girlfriends, boyfriends, pals and buddies. Enterprising restauranteurs latched on to the iconography of the diner luring us back to the places where we could relax and be ourselves. Suddenly, there were caboose restaurants, renovated lunchrooms, and flashy rebuilt diners that never came close to resembling the originals. Especially in the latter category, neon glitz and glitter abounded, gourmet meatloaf served with dijon mustard was presented on a platter stenciled "Blue Plate Special". Sexy waitresses decked out in bellboy caps and carhop skirts roller-skated over to your table to take an order.

It was all too cute for words. Striving so hard to recreate the diners of yesteryear seemed a bit odd as the diners of yesteryear—few though they may be—are still with us.

As confirmed purists, grumbling about tradition defiled and icons smashed comes with the turf. Indeed, we sometimes feel like Al Jolson's cantor father in "The Jazz Singer" who banished poor Al from the familial home because he had forsaken traditional Hebrew chant for jazz music. However, there is an up-side to all this diner revisionism going on. It lets those of us who eat know there is a grand tradition of dinering still in existence. Dinermen still practice grillmanship in those cozy archetectual gems everyday serving travelers and workers alike. In the following pages, we honor the great dinermen like Bosko, Gabe Moura, and John George— all unsung heros in the diner tradition who revere hard work, and a "good feed."

So come with us as we turn back the clock to today and drop in on the original "Counter Culture."

Late one winter night, we were driving home from a friend's wedding in Connecticut. We had eaten and drunk quite a bit during the day and still felt the effects of overindulgence. The roads were icy and dark and winding. If only we could stop for a cup of coffee and stretch our legs! Then, from out of nowhere, came the warm glow of a neon light, and we saw the word DINER.

It was a 1950s stainless steel affair, slightly run-down from years of use but basically well maintained. The inside was all pink and robin's-egg blue: the counter top and booths blue, the recessed ceiling a glowing pink. The place was brightly lighted by fluorescent lights. We were glad to be there.

There were no other customers. The waitress behind the counter sized us up quickly, and someone, perhaps the owner or a cook, gave us a perfunctory glance through one of the windows of the kitchen door and then disappeared forever.

When the waitress asked, "What'll it be, fellas?" we ordered coffee and apple pie. Looking around us, we realized how many times we had been in almost identical places and how much we felt right at home. We thought about Sunday dinners at the Ogantz Diner, and how the whole neighborhood would be there; we thought about breakfast at Skee's and late-night snacks at the Roslyn Diner. And we thought about the countless other diners we had stopped at, like the one we were in then, and how much they meant to us.

As we drank our steaming coffee from mugs, we talked with the waitress, who told us about favorite diners of her own. When we first walked in, there had been a moment of tension—after all, she was practically alone—but that soon

10 disappeared when she recognized us as just two more weary travelers.

We started talking about all the ways that we'd seen diners used: Norman Rockwell paintings, *I Love Lucy* episodes, innumerable stories and movies. We realized that diners are always there—people using them, feeling good about them—but rarely are they talked about, much less written about or taken seriously. We decided to do something about it. This, then, is our tribute to some of the great diners.

For the moment, put aside your greasy-spoon images. We have found most diners to have an atmosphere and a feel all their own. They are often run by husband-and-wife teams who keep the establishment as clean as a whistle and prepare the food as if it was going into the mouths of their own children (it usually does, as the offspring are almost always around, washing dishes or waiting tables). The prices for a home-cooked meal couldn't be cheaper, and the atmosphere is always relaxed and homey. And as if this weren't enough, the railroad-style architecture of the old diner is truly unique, found only in America. In all Europe, you will not find one diner; somehow, even the idea of a diner in France seems wrong.

When we say "diner" we have a specific type of eating place in mind. The word is used loosely. Frequently it refers to ordinary truck stops: luncheonettes, cafés, and plain old wooden shacks with neon EAT signs outside. These, to us, are not true diners. When we say "diner," we are referring to a building that was completely prefabricated in a factory and, until 1960, was designed in the style of a railroad car or trolley. The building was shipped to its site as one or two units on a flatbed truck, or by rail, or over the highway on its own wheels. When it reached its destination, the building was slid onto a foundation that contained the plumbing and the wiring. The final process, from shipping to connection of the electrical and water outlet, could take as little as forty-eight hours.

In the last two decades, diner manufacturers have turned away from the railroad car motif, favoring Mediterranean and colonial styles featuring fake marble, plastic statuary, and synthetic materials of dubious quality. Although we can appreciate certain aspects of these establishments and recognize, in some instances, the marble is not fake and the statuary is not plastic, we are referring here to the overall aesthetic values, rather than to the intrinsic quality of the materials or workmanship. New Jersey and Queens, New York, have become famous for this new kind of so-called diner. We follow the precepts of the great diner owner Gabe Moura, who says, "If you can't move it, it's not a diner."

The original diners had the grill behind the counter in full view of the patrons. Gabe feels, and we certainly would agree, that it is still almost essential for a true diner to have a grill up front, so that the customers may participate, at least as spectators, in the process of getting their food to the table. Modern-day diner/restaurants have completely done away with the grill up front. Sometimes we wonder what goes on back there in the kitchen.

The diner presents a real slice of American life. While it is not our purpose to indulge in instant sociology, we must note that a diner is one of the few places where doctors, lawyers, garbage collectors, and factory workers can be found sitting side by side. This form of "counter culture" was in existence long before the 1960s and is still alive and well at your local diner. The counter is the pulse and heartbeat of the diner. If you want a fix on any town and its people, just sit at the counter and take it all in. Stories, jokes, and one-liners old enough to be your grandfather's zip back and forth between regulars, waitresses, and countermen. Eavesdropping is definitely in order, and participation in any conversation is welcomed. In fact, many of the regulars count on talk from new faces to pass the time on what might otherwise be a dull day.

Next time you're in a diner, pay particular attention to the person working the grill. It's this worker's organizational skill and grace that determine the success of the operation. As we've said, the diner was originally built as one unit, with all the cooking facilities up front. Unlike a restaurant, where the kitchen is out back, the grillman is always on display. (A little note here: Many women work the grill, but the term "grillman" is traditionally accepted and serves to define any such person, regardless of gender; the same goes for "counterman" and "dinerman.") If the food hygiene is anything less than acceptable, the customer will see it. A number of grillmen we spoke with remarked on the pressure of having to prepare food in front of an audience. In fact, one grillman, at the Orchid Diner, mournfully recalled his experience with a customer who kept suggesting fifteen different ways to poach an egg. But if there are pressures on this job, there are also the high points that any performer feels. Some grillmen have developed bravura theatrics, such as cracking eggs two in each hand at breathtaking speed, flipping pancakes artfully into the air, or pouring pancake batter into the shape of prehistoric monsters for grade-schoolers on Saturday morning.

After years of practice in countering the remarks of customers, grillmen have also developed a repertoire of slick responses. They are masters of the glib, off-the-cuff put-down and have an arsenal of insults that would put Don Rickles to shame. This is done lightheartedly, for the most part. It's an indoor sport that helps make life in the diner that much more interesting.

Frequently, diner booths are the domain of families, tourists, salesmen, and retirees. And, yes, some waitresses still treat you like a close friend with a "dear" or a "hon" following every "What would you like?" In an area with a large elderly population, the booths often serve as a community center. In Rutland, Vermont, we heard a story about an older regular who was recovering from a recent operation. When he failed to show up one day, the waitress sent someone to check on him. On a day-to-day level, there is that kind of caring that goes beyond food.

Throughout the twentieth century, filmmakers and artists have been fascinated by the iconography of the diner. Who can forget—or resist—the opening scene of *Little Caesar,* where Edward G. Robinson sticks up the owner of a cute little greasy spoon? (If only we had been there to redirect Edward G's attention to the marvelous detail of the mosaic floor or the wonderful porcelain mugs. Possibly we could have engaged him in conversation, to ask if he knew of other diners in the area as nice as the one he was holding up.) More recently, Woody Allen not only featured a shot of the Empire Diner in his montage of New York in the movie "Manhattan" but continued to use the diner as a central prop in his later film "The Purple Rose of Cairo." And of course the film "Diner" featured a '50s style stainless steel beauty where the guys would meet after safely escorting their dates home.

One of our favorite screen diners is found in a vintage Popeye short, "We Aim to Please." In this early Max Fleischer cartoon, Popeye and Olive Oyl open their own diner and dance around the outside of their new restaurant while singing the title song. Of course, Bluto opens his own wagon across the way and a heavy competition ensues, with

Wimpy being the beneficiary of a hamburger price war.

Painters have also shown a fondness for the image of the diner. Norman Rockwell, the great chronicler of the American life-style, frequently used diners in his paintings. Edward Hopper, another American painter, spent a lifetime looking at the familiar and the forgotten. (He was a member of the Ashcan school of painting, which portrayed the grittier side of city life: the drugstores, factories, rows of brownstones, and all-night cafés.) The evocative and mysterious diner in Hopper's painting "Nighthawks" never fails to excite the imagination. Is the couple at the counter in love? Is the man with his back to us angry? Is the short-order cook toiling for the minimum wage?

With the advent of the Abstract Expressionist school of painting, the literal image of objects was shunned, put in the deep-freeze. But by the early 1970s, representational painting was back notably in the form of John Baeder's photo-realism. Baeder's paintings represent the most important contribution to the burgeoning field of diner art in that they focus on the entire diner experience. His wonderful book of paintings, *Diners* (Abrams, 1978), emphasizes the beauty of the diner's structure. Ralph Goings, another photo-realist, focuses primarily on diner interiors and still lifes.

In the field of crafts, Harry Cavanagh makes ceramic diner butter dishes in his upstate New York studio. We've even seen a line of diner throw pillows.

Television has not been immune to the fascination of the original fast-food restaurant. Diners have been featured in several TV shows, most notably *Alice,* where virtually all the action occurs in Mel's Diner. And there's one early episode of *I Love Lucy* where Lucy and Ricky join Fred and Ethel in another of their ill-fated business partnerships, and all chip in to buy a diner.

Diners have been prefabricated since the first commercially made structure appeared in the late nineteenth century. Not a nail or rivet was missing from any part of the building when it reached its site. Even dishes, silverware, and wall menus were supplied by the manufacturer, creating a complete operation, ready on arrival to amass large profits—the ideal American business.

The old diners were designed in the *style* of a dining car, which earlier in this century was considered the height of elegance, but contrary to popular belief, they were not actual railroad cars themselves. The railroad-car motif has permeated our architectural landscape. While the diner is the primary example, the influence of this mode of design can be seen in mobile homes, buses, and other moving vehicles. Combining motion and elegance in a stationary restaurant was an ingenious idea. For the average customer, it offered the illusion of getting away from it all in comfort and style—in other words, of taking a vacation on your lunch break.

We found a concern for personal contact running through every phase of diner development and design. This is a by-product of what is called vernacular architecture. Those who usually designed diners were not architects but more likely the chief engineer or president of the manufacturing company. As is often the case with minds unfettered by the rules of an academy, these men came up with innovative and sophisticated plans. With no formal background in design, they drew upon the familiar and the comfortable: the family kitchen, the parlor, the trolley and railroad car. They took from what they saw around them, and this helped to create the diner's feeling of warmth. Nowhere is the cold pragmatism of an architectural firm to be found.

A good deal of myth and misinformation surrounds our ideas about diners, partly because no one has ever bothered to document the diner phenomenon. There is little in the way of printed matter on the subject. A notable exception is *American Diner* (Harper & Row, 1979), a study of the historical and social aspects of diners by Richard Gutman and Elliott Kaufman (written in collaboration with David Slovic). However, much of what we ourselves learned came from short-order cooks and diner owners—men like Bosko, of Bosko's Diner in South River, New Jersey; Frank Tinelli of the Suburban Skyliner in Polksville, New York; and John George, who owns the Boulevard Diner in Worcester, Massachusetts—men who have lived and worked in diners since the 1930s and know every aspect of "dinerology," from the early wagons to their modern-day counterparts. Because ours is an oral history, it becomes difficult to verify actual dates. The only help we had was from manufacturers' records, various articles in books and magazines, and a trade publication, *Diner* magazine. The following account represents a synthesis of these oral and written sources.

In 1872 it was almost impossible to find a restaurant anywhere that was open after 8:00 P.M. Walter Scott, of Providence, Rhode Island, took advantage of this unhappy situation when he began loading a horse-drawn wagon with pies, sandwiches, and coffee and rolling it downtown to Journal Square at dusk. This was the first lunch wagon, predecessor of the diner. Much to his delight, Scotty found a hungry and enthusiastic public out there. Other enterprising businessmen quickly took up the idea, and these wagons, called "night owls," began springing up all over New England. Soon the menu was expanded to include hot dogs, beans, and cold cuts, and so the "dog wagon" was born. Within the next ten years, the number of wagons in Providence alone grew to thirty.

By the late 1880s, the wagon business was booming. Most carts were custom-made by local blacksmiths or wagon builders, but by 1887, Ruel B. Jones, also of Providence, began manufacturing more elaborate ones. These wagons had such features as etched windows, hand-painted exteriors, and more sophisticated cooking equipment. Not to be outdone, the Church Temperance Society got into the act, opening a series of wagons in New York City as an alternative to the ever-present gin mill and thus giving some respectability to the "night owl."

In the year 1891, Charles H. Palmer of Worcester, Massachusetts, applied for the first diner patent. He called his wagons "Night Owl Lunches"; some old-timers today still refer to diners as "night owls." But it took Thomas H. Buckley, the "lunch wagon king," to bring diners into their own. His factory in Worcester was the largest diner manufactory to that date, employing eighty workers. Buckley extended the width of the average diner from six to ten feet to create a more comfortable dining area, and he paid attention to aesthetics by incorporating nickel-plated coffee urns and stools. Exteriors were lovingly decorated with gold scrolls on bas-relief against a white background.

In 1897, Boston, Philadelphia, and New York junked their horse-drawn trolleys and replaced them with new electric models. Local merchants bought the old trolley cars for fifteen or twenty dollars and converted them to lunch cars. But these old, delapidated trolleys were hardly the place where you would want to eat a quick lunch, let alone take your family for Sunday dinner, and before long an undesirable element started frequenting them. The appearance of these dingy, drafty diners was unfortunate, because two myths arose which have never been dispelled: that diners are converted railroad cars and that they are seedy, low-class joints. Indeed, the good citizens of Buffalo and Atlantic City went so far as to ban them by city ordinance.

Luckily, Patrick J. ("Pop") Tierney came along in the early part of this century and rehabilitated the diner to new respectability. Among other claims to fame, Pop was known as the man who brought the toilet inside. He also shrewdly introduced the concept of the booth, so that women who considered sitting on a stool at a counter unladylike might dine in one of his establishments in comfort. In an effort to create a new image of elegance, Tierney looked to the railroad dining car as his design model. This inspired the introduction of a line of small windows and a barreled roof. All these innovations helped to attract family dining.

What really cinched the inevitability of diner growth was the invention of the automobile and the resulting vast network of highways. People took to the road in droves. They had to eat somewhere, and diners were ideal. They could easily be placed anywhere, and they offered quick service at reasonable prices. (One reason diners were transformed from wagons to stationary restaurants was that wagons were constantly being ticketed by local constables. Once the wheels were removed, however, diner owners were no longer subject to traffic laws.)

During the 1920s the miracle metal Monel was introduced from Germany. It appeared in railroad cars around 1924 and was soon adopted for use in diners. Monel, a sleek and shiny nickel alloy used for grill hoods, design trim, canopies, and kick plates for swinging doors, was the forerunner of stainless steel. It never lost its shine and could take a tremendous beating without chipping. The Worcester Lunch Car Company used this metal in their diners in the late 1920s and into the '30s.

The Worcester Lunch Car Company could itself be the subject of an entire book. Our dream of seeing this legendary manufacturing plant in full operation was brought as close to reality as possible when we had the good fortune to run into Saul Talbert, who owns the building that once housed the now-defunct company. Mr. Talbert took us on a tour of the plant. He showed us the small balconies where workers would fashion parts before they were brought down into the barn and placed inside the diner. We saw outlines in the brick exterior of the building of doors wide enough for a finished diner to be hauled through. We went upstairs, sat in what was the lounge/locker room, and looked at first-aid cabinets and cubbyholes built right into the walls—used for who knows what. We went into the foreman's office: the big, old oak double-sided desk was still there, as was the original office safe. We looked into what was the main office, still intact, with its oak walls and counter and tiled floor. All this was manna from heaven to us.

The Worcester Lunch Cars were some of the warmest and coziest diners built. The construction process was a layered one, starting with a rectangular steel frame built on a set of wheels. Then different teams of workers applied their various skills to the bare structure. First came the interior crew, who filled the frame with twenty-gauge steel. Electrical and plumbing work was next, followed by oak or mahogany paneling for the walls. The masonry was done by an Italian crew, who showed an amazing amount of care for detail in the hand-tiled mosaic floors and counter bases. After the cooking equipment was installed, large sheets of porcelain enamel were layered on the exterior. Finally, the name of the establishment was hand-painted on the building's front, in Gothic script. (Such was the dedication of these workers, reported the *Worcester Telegram*, that during the auction sale which followed the closing of the company in

1961, many of the older crew members were seen trying to hold back their tears as a way of life literally ended before their very eyes.)

For fifty-six years, these meticulously crafted cars, unique in their look and feel, filled every nook and cranny of New England. The guiding light of the Worcester Lunch Car Company was Charles Gemme, who was with the company from its inception in 1906 until it finally closed its doors in the early 1960s. Dick Gutman told us he had tried to interview Gemme, but the man was already in his nineties and provided little real information. It seems that Gemme was dinered out and had lost much of his enthusiasm for the subject. What a frustrating experience this must have been, as though one had access to the Rosetta stone but no means of deciphering it. Worcester Lunch Cars remain among our favorite diners, and whenever we eat in one we feel comfortable enough to be at home.

More diners were built from the 1920s through the 1940s than at any other time. Again, this had to do with the expansion of roadways. Although Pop Tierney's company declined, new manufacturers sprouted up and set the tone of the diner business for the next thirty years.

Jerry O'Mahony, Paramount, Silk City (also known as the Patterson Vehicle Company), Worcester, Sterling, Mountain View, and Manno were the major manufacturers, along with Kullman and De Raffele, who still make modern diners. Other companies, both major and minor in size, are presently manufacturing contemporary diners. Most used a barreled roof in their design. O'Mahony and Worcester favored the style of the pointed monitor roof, which they took directly from the trolley. These roofs added height and made diners feel roomier. The barrel roof and the use of stainless steel were the beginning of the streamlined look that many people now associate with diners. Most true diners remaining today are from this Golden Age of diner production.

The 1950's and 1960's brought a radical change in design. Harold Kullman Jr. of the Kullman Dining Car Co., along with the De Raffele Manufacturing Co., were among the first diner manufacturers to use the Colonial style we see today. The Mediterranean and Spanish Mission design followed featuring gaudy interiors and an ersatz-look to almost everything. Even if we don't agree with the taste of these manufacturers, they knew what they were doing. They foresaw the expansion of the fastfood chain, and the public's desire for a more modern place to eat as a challenge to meet. Their new concept of the diner as a restaurant, with the grill banished to the back out of the customers' sight, caught on with the dining public looking for something new. Fast-food chains further contributed to the demise of the old-fashioned diner by offering plastic food in plastic surroundings, served with all the personal contact of a plastic clown. With a sense of gratitude we notice an ever-deepening backlash against these franchises and hope it will rekindle an interest in the old lunch car.

You may notice that every diner in this book is located in the Northeast. The reason for this is simple: The Northeast is where the diner originated, where it is still manufactured, and where it is most commonly found (although one may occasionally stumble across a lunch wagon west of the Mississippi). The Northeastern United States is the cradle of diner civilization.

Some proprietors refused to believe that anyone would write a diner book and insisted that we were IRS agents or spies from McDonald's. Most, however, were flattered to talk about their experiences, just as you would respond to anyone who showed a true interest in your work.

Dinermen are a special breed. They are not chefs or restaurateurs, and they'll be insulted if you refer to them as such. They're *dinermen,* proud of their tradition and fighting hard to preserve their way of life in the face of the fast-food incursion. In an effort to understand the world of the diner, we interviewed countless diner owners, grillmen, waitresses, dishwashers, and regular customers over endless cups of coffee. What resulted was a mosaic of life stories that were sometimes exciting, frequently touching, and always interesting.

Many diner owners we spoke with are saddened when young children walk into their places and act as though they were on another planet. They tug at Mom or Dad's sleeve and beg them to go to the place that has the picture of the clown on the glass and serves the burgers in bright-colored cardboard boxes. Many's the time we heard the word "brainwashed" from a diner owner or worker when referring to the effect that fast-food advertising has had on these kids.

We should warn all of you who use this book that the search for the perfect diner can become addictive. Travel to one, and the patrons or owner will wax ecstatic about another. Before you know it, you've driven another ten miles out of your way to sample some fine chowder or see a vintage Worcester car. Or maybe you're just driving down the road and you sight a silver diner in the distance. Your pulse quickens as you feel the thrill of discovery, a stainless steel secret that's all your own. As you stand in the parking lot, the pleasing aroma of diner food assails your nostrils and you can almost feel your fingers wrapped around that heavy coffee mug. You wonder whom you will meet inside and what new experiences you will find in what we call the "counter culture."

Eating at a diner is an experience that brings us back to an America that had time to sit down and eat a home-cooked meal at leisure. The service may be quick, but you are rarely hurried out (unless, of course, it's lunchtime, when everybody's in a hurry). The atmosphere may not be fancy, and sometimes the food may be overcooked, but it's made by human hands that care. It's a diner, with a feel all its own.

# Connecticut

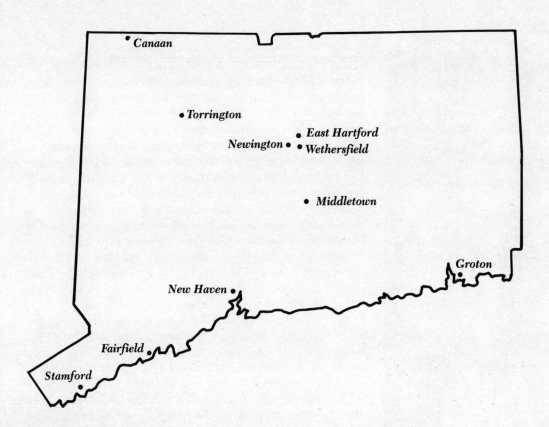

- Canaan
- Torrington
- East Hartford
- Newington • Wethersfield
- Middletown
- Groton
- New Haven
- Fairfield
- Stamford

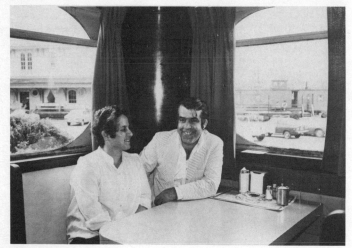

*The Hamzys*

## Collin's Diner

*Canaan, Connecticut*

When Collin's Diner was written up in the *New York Times* some four years ago, the response was terrific. Mike Hamzy, the owner, told us that the place was packed with strange faces, and his business is usually 90 percent regulars. The article brought in a host of celebrities, all of whom came to see a "real diner." Paul Newman, the Smothers Brothers, Loretta Swit, Farrah Fawcett, and Lee Majors have come to eat in this family-oriented establishment.

Collin's was built in 1941 in Elizabeth, New Jersey. Mike's a diner afficionado and has kept everything the same since he purchased it from the original owner some fifteen years ago. Perhaps the most striking feature is the marble counter. One day a professor from M.I.T., eating at this counter, discovered that it was full of rare fossils. He offered to buy it and replace it with a new one, but he was turned down.

Mike tries to serve only fresh foods in his diner. In the summer months all the vegetables are fresh and are grown locally. He even has his own gardens, which last year yielded 110 pounds of asparagus. Other fresh vegetables include tomatoes, corn, green beans, and squash.

There are breakfast, luncheon, and dinner specials every day. The 99-cent breakfast is two eggs, toast, and coffee—no potatoes, since Mike claims he pays extra for his farm-fresh eggs, but you do get extra cups of coffee free. With breakfast meats the price shoots way up, to over $2.00. The eggs are cooked only in butter, unless you request otherwise.

The luncheon special costs about $1.50. Franks and beans, American chop suey, meat loaf, and stuffed cabbage are some of the offerings. They all come with bread and butter, a vegetable, and mashed potato and all are prepared to be served quickly.

The most expensive dinner specials run about $5.00, and that would be the ham steak, the fried scallops, or the jumbo shrimp. A hot beef sandwich costs about $3.50. Other specials are the breaded veal and the southern fried chicken. The scallops are fresh, but the fried clams are not; they are frozen clam strips supplied by the S. S. Pierce Company.

Most of the soups—beef noodle, chicken rice, and split pea, to name a few—are homemade. If Mike has to open a can, he'll let you know.

Collin's makes its own dessert puddings: bread, rice, and custard. When we were there, Table Top pies were being served, but plans were under way to buy fresh-baked pies from a local woman.

Mike feels that people who pay money to eat in his diner have the right to see how the food is prepared. Not only does he do much of the cooking up front, on the grill, but his kitchen is always open for inspection. He once answered a customer's question—whether the spaghetti came out of a can—by taking him back to the kitchen and showing him the huge pot of freshly made spaghetti sauce. Mike makes twenty-six quarts of tomato sauce twice weekly, and he makes his own meatballs too.

Collin's Diner takes a lot of pride in good service. Regular customers know their breakfast will be on the grill, and their coffee on the counter, as soon as they're spied in the parking lot. Mike has a promise that he makes to all customers. If you walk into his diner and you're the only customer, it's a free meal. The chances of this happening are slim.

Canaan is at the southern end of the Berkshire Hills, and it's beautiful country. Collin's is located right next to the old Canaan train station, which has been converted to commercial use since passenger service was discontinued. The foothills of the Berkshires serve as the diner's backdrop. Mike loves the diner just as it is. He feels that people come to eat in diners because the food is fresh, the price is right, and they like the way diners look. To add a dining room, he says, would destroy the structure. He told us that he "wouldn't add an inch."

A little aside that we found interesting is that Mike learned to cook while working in a restaurant owned by consumer advocate Ralph Nader's father.

## Mark Twain Diner ===================

*East Hartford, Connecticut*

================================

The Mark Twain is a transitional diner. It was designed before they stopped making diners that look like diners, but after they moved the grill from behind the counter into the kitchen. For us, the grill out front is one of the things that makes a diner a diner, but the feel, the style, and the food at the Mark Twain are reason enough to include it in this book.

Built about 1960 by the Masters Company, with huge windows around all sides, the color scheme of the Mark Twain is predominantly pink. The counter seats twelve. There are five booths along the wall opposite the counter and four more, as well as a horseshoe-shaped booth, in an adjoining dining area.

The owner of the Mark Twain, Philip Vrakas, is part of the new tradition of Greek diner owners. He does virtually everything in this twenty-four-hour diner himself, buying, cooking, and serving with very little help, often putting in a sixteen-hour day. It's his personal attention that is responsible for the high quality of what's offered.

This is the only diner we visited that has a salad bar. Philip had to remove a booth to make room for it, and it's a most welcome addition. In the evenings you can make all the salad you wish with your dinner.

There are two different menus—one for the daytime and one for night. The reason for this is that the diner attracts a large after-bar crowd at night. Not only are these people more difficult to deal with, but they sometimes forget to pay their bills. So Philip sets out a separate menu, with slightly higher prices, to compensate for the higher level of aggravation he has to deal with.

Two dishes that are offered only on the night menu are steak and eggs and pastrami and eggs. For some reason, there seems to be more of a call for these platters late at night. The steak is an eight-ounce sirloin and costs about $5.00. The pastrami and eggs will run you about $2.50.

The Mark Twain is located across the street from an aircraft factory that employs thirty thousand workers. Like the diner, the factory works around the clock, and many of the employees come into the Mark Twain for lunch. Philip makes everything fresh. We asked about the neon sign advertising seafood in the diner's window and were told that he gets his fish fresh from a local dealer several times a week. It's usually halibut or flounder. Philip also gets whole clams for his chowder, which he serves on Fridays. He alternates, from week to week, between Manhattan and New England chowder.

During the week there's a soup-and-sandwich special offered at lunchtime. The sandwiches are usually some sort of salad, such as ham salad or tuna salad. The soups, all homemade, include chicken rice, navy bean, and minestrone. The $1.35 price for the special includes a cup of coffee.

Daily specials are offered until 8:30 each evening. The top price for one of these dishes is about $3.25. One night it might be Hungarian goulash or half a roast chicken. Occasionally, Philip makes a Greek specialty, like moussaka, a meat and eggplant dish. These platters come with potato and a vegetable or salad. Other specials include Yankee pot roast, meat loaf, and baked sausage.

All the muffins—corn, bran, blueberry, and pineapple—are baked on the premises and are square-shaped. Philip also make the apple pie and a large selection of puddings: tapioca, rice, bread, and grape nut.

In talking about his fast-food competition, Philip used that key word many diner owners use: "brainwashing." He feels that the TV commercials kids see program them to drag Mom and Dad into quick-service burger joints that offer soda glasses with clown pictures. These kids have no patience with diners. This was strange to us, who remember fondly, from our childhood, being taken to a gleaming diner for dinner and always running into our friends and neighbors while we were there.

We asked Philip if his diner was called the Mark Twain because Hartford boasts, as a historical landmark, the home of the father of the modern American novel. No, he said, it was carrying this name when he took it over from a cousin. He wasn't aware of who the real Mark Twain might have been.

## Larry's Diner

*Fairfield, Connecticut*

We arrived at Larry's Diner just at closing time on a Saturday afternoon. The last few customers were finishing their meals, and owner Bob Convertito and his help were cleaning up. There's a certain moment when a diner stops. The customers are gone; the clatter of plates dies down. There's a strange stillness, the lingering odor of food, a heightened awareness of the wooden booths and the tiled floor and the barreled roof. The quiet of closing is broken only by the sound of change being counted. All this is a part of the diner experience.

If you're looking for a real old-time diner that's just a short drive from New York, Larry's is a must. It was built in 1928 by the O'Mahony Company and brought into Fairfield by rail. The wheels were attached directly to an axle at the base of the building, and it was rolled off the siding and pulled into town just like a trailer. Back then it had the same sit-down counter and a stand-up rail along the windows. In 1936 it was moved one block to its present location and was widened by the manufacturer, in order to keep the same look and feel. A kitchen annex was added at the same time.

There has been virtually no change in the appearance of Larry's in over forty years. The counter top is marble, and the interior is all wood with a mahogany veneer. The grill

*Original bun warmer. Name plate reads, "Jerry O'Mahony Inc., Dining Car Builders, Elizabeth, N.J."*

hood, which is kept highly polished, is nickel-plated copper, and the wood-framed menu boards are fastened to the ceiling with brass rods. There's a tremendous amount of fine detail work throughout Larry's, and it's obvious that great care went into its design and manufacture. Be sure to check out the chrome bun warmer that still carries on its front the brass plate with the manufacturer's name.

Bob is a heavy-set, ex-physical therapist in his thirties, and he and his wife do most of the work. There's a lot involved in keeping the place running six days a week. Bob grew up in the area around Fairfield, and he enjoys seeing people whom he hasn't seen in years come in as customers. The original owner was a Larry Doyle, and the story goes that he lost the diner to its second owner, Charlie Kadar, in a poker game. Back when Charlie owned it, he had a deaf counterman named Pete who used to turn off his hearing aid and just read lips when he didn't want to be bothered.

Most of the clientele at Larry's are regular customers, and Bob says they all love the diner because of its age and beauty. We're sure the freshness of the food, and its preparation, has something to do with the diner's popularity. We especially liked the clam chowder, which was loaded with chunks of fresh clam meat and pieces of celery. The hot dogs were the largest we've ever seen—the size of knockwurst—and there's a sandwich called a quarter-pound hot dog. This quarter-pounder includes bacon, melted cheese, sauerkraut, and fried onions. It's a meal in itself.

Breakfast is the biggest meal at Larry's. Since the diner first opened, the eggs have come from the same place, Sargent's Egg Farm. Sarge, who delivers the eggs himself, is a tall, slender seventy-year-old. Whenever he comes in he loves to pester the waitresses, and no matter what they say or do, they just can't insult him. One waitress at another diner hauled off and hit him with a pie one day, but it didn't faze Sarge in the least; he was back the following day, acting true to form.

Bob told us that his morning customers seem to come in shifts. First, at opening time, there are the factory workers and cops, then come the town workers—road crews, and the like—and then the doctors on their way to the hospital and business people on their way to work. There's a lot of sports talk at all hours, especially during the baseball season, because the fans around there are pretty evenly divided between the Red Sox and the Yankees. There are even a couple of oversized baseballs hanging from the ceiling at the far end of the counter.

Larry's, the only diner we ever encountered with a white picket fence around it, is located on Route 1, which runs right through Fairfield and used to be the only way you could get there. Nowadays it's easier to take Interstate 95, but our hearts are still with the old road, which was once a great diner trail.

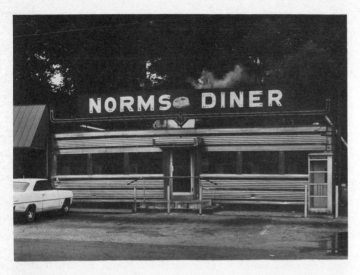

*Norman Broche*

*Groton, Connecticut*

Norms Diner could be the last Silk City diner with a barreled roof. Built in 1954, its curved gray-and-white Formica ceiling creates a polar atmosphere. Sitting at a booth, the view through the window is of the nearby Thames River and the mammoth Gold Star Memorial Bridge. Norman Broche, the owner of the diner, greeted us wearing a shirt decorated with pictures of the Statue of Liberty and other New York landmarks. It made us just a little bit homesick.

Groton is a seaport and the home of one of the nation's largest nuclear submarine bases and manufacturing centers. A few days before our visit to the diner, there had been an anti–nuclear-power demonstration in town. Norm, who depends on the industry for much of his business and is friendly with many of the workers and sailors, wasn't fazed by the sight of the thousands of demonstrators, quite a few of whom came into the diner to eat. As a matter of fact, Norm, a lanky six-footer in his early forties, seemed as though very few things would excite him.

The inside of the diner is filled with dark green: The booths and stools are upholstered in green, and the base of the counter is tiled in two shades of green, with a thin strip of pink running across its length. The tile on the floor is green, and the soup cups and saucers have a green tint. The table and counter tops are pink Formica, and a strip of pink runs above the mirrors at the far end of the counter and the windows.

Norms Diner serves a full selection of fish, even though Norm himself admits to hating it. We thought that was unusual, since it can be difficult to cook something well that you yourself don't like, but we found the fish to be particularly fresh and tasty, even though we didn't get fresh lemon with it.

The regular menu lists a few fish selections, like fish-and-chips, fried scallops, and oysters. It states that seafood is available in season, so check the blackboard behind the counter to see what's being offered that day. You might find striped bass stuffed with scallops, shrimp and bread crumbs, or maybe fried smelts in the spring. There's also finnan haddie (smoked cod) in the fall, and yellowtail flounder. Norm told us that he fries his fish in what is called a dry batter, which is thin, not doughy or greasy. He uses a thicker, or wet, batter when he makes his chicken fried steak (a fried chicken cutlet), because it holds more of the juices, which is important with chicken.

There are several specials each day. We tried the chicken cutlets, which are deep-fried strips of chicken, and found them moist and flavorful. They were served with homemade mashed potatoes, which are made with butter and are quite good. The whole thing was covered with a rich brown gray that Norm himself makes. Also available are liver and bacon, grilled ham steak, and an open steak sandwich.

Norm makes all his own soups. We had the chicken gumbo, which was served in a cup on a saucer. (The soup may come in a cup, but the coffee's served in a mug, which we like because it keeps the coffee hotter longer.) The chicken gumbo was chock-full of chunks of chicken and pieces of celery, corn, rice, and tomato. The coleslaw is commercial but very good.

Breakfast is a big meal for Norm, who claims that folks will travel miles just to taste his home fries. We didn't get a chance to try them ourselves, so we'll just have to take his word for it.

There is a large selection of newspapers for sale, a very old candy machine, and a cigarette machine that sold us a particularly fresh pack of Camels.

Norm comes from a diner family. His father owned an old wooden Silk City that was just down the road from where he is now. Our hearts sank when he told us how bulldozers came in and knocked the place down after the property was sold.

Norm owns the entire block on which his diner stands, and he intends to build an adjoining restaurant and lounge. He'll leave the diner intact, although he's considering putting a connecting door between the two places. We hope the addition doesn't spoil the feel, and Norm has assured us it won't.

Groton is the home of at least one celebrity, Ruth Buzzi, who came to prominence on the TV show *Laugh-In*. Norm told us that she ate there regularly when she was growing up and that she still stops by whenever she's in town.

## O'Rourke's Diner

*Middletown, Connecticut*

People frequently ask us, "What's the best meal you had in the diners you visited?" We think about all the different diners and the broad array of foods we've been served. The coleslaw at Bosko's Diner, the clam stew at the Miss Portland, the stuffed chicken at Tommy's Deluxe—all excellent. But it might be that the steamed cheeseburgers and birch beer at O'Rourke's was our favorite meal, whether in a diner or not.

The owner of O'Rourke's is Brian O'Rourke, who is in his late twenties and is the nephew of the original owner of this 1946 Mountain View diner. The diner itself is a real beauty and has been kept in its original condition: blue and white tiles along the base of the marble counter, white enameled ceiling trimmed with blue, and glass brick by the front door. Fifteen green stools stand along the counter, and six green and blue booths provide additional seating. The doors to the phone and the rest rooms are a deep mahogany, and frosted glass panes top side windows overlooking train tracks that run next to and below the diner. When the freight train rolls by, the building rattles slightly, like a vibrating bed that takes quarters in a motel.

Brian started working in his uncle's diner when he was ten years old, coming in after school to peel potatoes. Later he started working weekends, and during high school he was working forty-five to fifty hours a week. Now, as owner, he works eighty or ninety hours a week and consumes at least thirty cups of coffee a day. "A lot of people say I work crazy hours, and I do," says Brian. "I work some weeks eighty, ninety, ninety-five hours. But ninety-five percent of the eighty hours you enjoy, because you're talkin' sports, or you're tellin' stories, or you're tellin' jokes. It's not a job."

The specialty of O'Rourke's is the steamed cheeseburger, an invention of another Middletown eatery, now defunct, where Brian's uncle once worked. The steamed cheeseburger is served in one or two other spots in town too.

O'Rourke's uses only top-quality cheese and meat. The cheese, used also on hot apple pie, franks, or even breakfast eggs, is the same New York cheddar that O'Rourke's has been buying for forty years. It comes in forty-pound wheels and must be at least one year old. Tasted fresh off the wheel, the cheese is sharp and rich in flavor; once it's been melted down into a delicious goo inside the steam box, some of the sharpness is smoothed out but all the flavor is left in.

The steam box, which stands about two feet high and is eighteen inches deep, looks a lot like an old bread box. There are racks inside the box, where the meat and cheese are placed in metal trays about the size of a playing card. Water goes in the bottom, and the whole thing sits over a burner that boils the water and steams the burger meat. The process is very simple, but years of practice go into making every burger taste just right. The steamed cheeseburger is best eaten on a roll with mustard and onion and washed down with some of the excellent soda that the diner offers. A hamburger served with onion is called a hamburg "trilby." Anything served with onion was once called a trilby. So at O'Rourke's you could ask for a ham trilby or a fried-egg sandwich trilby or anything else that comes to mind.

The birch beer, which is clear soda, is the best we've tasted in years. Served in an old-style long-necked bottle, it's a local product, Undina brand. The soda is made from sparkling spring water and is very refreshing. We also tried the Undina ginger ale and it was not too sweet, just right. Even the Coca-Cola that O'Rourke's carries is different from Coke available elsewhere. Brian gets the soda that's bottled in the small, thick-glass bottles. He pays a 15-cent deposit on each bottle because the thick glass helps create a better-tasting product. When the wall of the bottle is so strong, it can take a greater amount of pressure. Coke that goes into these bottles has much more fizz than soda that comes out of a thin can. Because it's bottled at a higher pressure, it has greater carbonation and a livelier taste.

Of course, Brian serves other things besides burgers, but other than the homemade breakfast muffins, almost everything else is a sandwich or an omelette. There are no soups or platters in this twenty-four-hour diner. The big attraction is that it's very much a diner, a place where all sorts of people come together from all walks of life. And O'Rourke's encourages this in many ways. For example, there are always ten different newspapers available for customers every day, including the New York and Boston dailies as well as local papers. We thought this was a nice touch.

To Brian, the diner is a special place, and he has high regard for his customers. "A diner is a completely different way of life," he told us. "It's like everything molded into one. Some mornings you might have a doctor sitting here, you might have a lawyer sitting here, you might have two college kids, you might have some hooker over in a booth, you might have a guy here who could buy and sell the whole place. It's true. You could take a picture at ten o'clock some morning. It's a crossroads. Everybody feels at home."

Brian told us about the habits of some of the regular customers. Some people act like clocks for him. "A lot of people sit in the same booth at exactly the same time," he explained. "I could tell what time of day it is by who's in here. I could wake up out of a trance, not knowing if I had slept one hour or twenty hours, and if you put me right here and just opened my eyes, and if I looked in that corner and saw Hal Morgan I'd know it would be eight o'clock. If I looked over and saw my father, I'd know it would be seven thirty. If I saw the girl from across the street, I'd know it would be ten o'clock. It's like a part of your life. It's like looking that way is the clock."

The counter as clock. This was a new addition to what we call the "counter culture," life on both sides of the counter.

The diner also puts out a weekly newsletter, which is a few pages of pleasant name-dropping. It's mailed out to all those Middletowners who are laid up or out of town or who for some other reason cannot take part in the town's social life but still like to keep in touch with what's going on.

The combination of architecture, pride in the quality of food and service, and the real part that the diner plays in the life of the town make O'Rourke's a true diner experience.

## Hi-Way Diner

*New Haven, Connecticut*

Because of the old axiom "For good food, follow the truckers," we wound up at the Hi-Way Diner. There's nothing fancy about this white and gray Mountain View diner, just good solid food at reasonable prices.

Mike Apazidis, the owner, is a young Greek who bought the Hi-Way from his cousin early in 1979. Mike told us that he'd been in the restaurant business ever since he arrived from Greece seven years ago. He takes pride in being a diner owner and tries to please his customers by keeping the food simple and the diner clean.

The Hi-Way was built about twenty-five years ago, and although the color scheme is predominantly gray and white, the base of the Formica counter is pink, as is the lower part of the walls. Large curved windows go all the way around the building, even at the corners.

Frequently, a Greek diner owner will put a dish or two from his native land on the menu, so we asked Mike if he ever does that. He told us he avoids it; he wants "nothing that anybody doesn't know what it is. Nothing fancy." In talking about the Hi-Way, which is located in a completely industrial part of New Haven and has obviously seen better days, Mike explained, "A long time ago this was a fancy diner for the people. Things change."

Mike certainly knows the diner business—and the diners.

We couldn't mention a diner in the state that he hadn't been to, and he told us about a few we weren't familiar with. You might think it is usual for someone in the business to be aware of others in the same line of work. Not true. We met many diner owners who didn't know what the inside of the diner in the next town looked like, let alone the next county. But Mike has a real feel for diners, and he enjoys stopping in to see what others are doing.

A big feature of the Hi-Way is the charcoal broiler. We always prefer the flavor of a charcoal-broiled steak or burger, and the burgers at the Hi-Way are particularly thick and juicy.

The breakfast special was an excellent buy when we stopped there. You will have to remember that inflation will make these prices somewhat higher, but for 95 cents Mike was offering a complete breakfast—two eggs, home fries, toast, and one cup of coffee. Bacon or sausage was another 60 cents. The price was the same for breakfast pancakes.

Mike told us he doesn't like foods that come from cans, and he makes his own soups from scratch. A partial listing of the ones served includes Yankee bean, beef barley, Manhattan clam chowder, and minestrone. These were priced at 45 cents a cup, 65 cents a bowl.

Some of the daily platter specials are franks and beans, roast beef, and liver steak. All these are reasonably priced. The liver steak platter, which includes salad, potato, vegetable, and a cup of coffee, cost slightly over $2.50. Bagels are available, there's homemade rice pudding, and coffee was modestly priced at 25 cents a cup. It's Martinson brand coffee, and particularly good.

The view from the Hi-Way is of a city made up of pale-pink-colored oil refinery tanks. While we were seated at a booth, we observed a yellow Coupe de Ville pull up outside, framed against the backdrop of the oil tanks. When the driver came into the diner and removed his black topcoat and hat before sitting at the counter, we couldn't help but notice his pale-green suit, yellow tuxedo shirt, and black tie. We asked Mike if he knew who it was. He told us that quite a few cops patronize his place and that this was a retired detective. For a brief moment we felt as though we had walked into the middle of a Frank Sinatra movie.

We found the Hi-Way to be a friendly place. When we asked for directions, several of the other customers got involved in trying to help us out. The diner is easily accessible from Interstate 95, going east. If you're traveling to or from New England, it's a good place to stop for a hearty meal or a fine cup of coffee.

*"World's longest diner"*

## Olympia Diner

*Newington, Connecticut*

The Olympia Diner could be the world's longest diner. It's so big that we expected to see the waitresses on roller skates, but no such luck. It certainly must have the world's largest diner parking lot.

Like its nearby neighbor in Wethersfield, the Makris Diner, the Olympia, is an O'Mahony. No one was sure just when it was built (we figure about thirty years ago), but we were told it was built as one unit, not two diners put end to end. The counter is twenty-one stools long, and in addition to the fifteen regular booths, there are two large horseshoe-shaped booths and a small dining annex with several long, banquet-style tables. The color scheme is green: green terrazzo floor, green stools, green walls with stainless steel trim, and green tabletops with inlaid yellow racing stripes.

We spoke with the manager, John Gineo, a slight, soft-spoken man who has been in the restaurant and baking business for over thirty years. John told us that when the diner was brought to its current location it came in three pieces that snapped together to make one unit.

The menu at the Olympia is quite extensive. As a matter of fact, befitting the world's longest diner, it could be the world's longest diner menu. Space prohibits a complete listing of the foods offered, but we will give you a partial one. We won't give the individual prices, but the cost is what we'd call reasonable—not really inexpensive, but reasonable.

Under the heading "Entrées" we found twenty-one different selections. There are also separate listings for "Broiled Steaks and Chops" and "Sea Food." Under entrées, there are London broil, leg of lamb, pot roast, roast turkey, corned beef hash with eggs, and roast fresh ham with applesauce, all served with potatoes and a vegetable or salad. Baked manicotti, baked lasagna, and franks and beans are served with salad only. All the roasts are real, full-sized roasts; the roast turkey is a whole turkey.

Among the broiled steaks and chops are a half broiled chicken, Virginia ham steak with Hawaiian pineapple ring, lamb chops, pork chops, and filet mignon. Like the entrées, these are served with potatoes and a vegetable or salad.

The seafood selection boasts of broiled scallops, fried shrimp in a basket, broiled trout, and salmon steak, among others. The fish is frozen and comes with the customary potatoes and a vegetable or salad.

There's a full salad selection, including a chicken salad platter and a chef's salad, as well as plenty of sandwiches. You will find eight different three-decker club sandwiches listed. Hot open-face sandwiches and hot oven grinders are offered. A steak grinder and an egg and pepper grinder are among the twelve types offered. In addition to all this, there are daily specials. With such a selection, how can you go wrong?

One of the first things you'll notice upon entering the Olympia is the large pastry refrigerator, with its glass doors, that's behind the counter. All baked goods are made on the premises, including the dinner and sandwich rolls. Desserts include such treats as chocolate éclairs, cream pies, apple turnovers, Danish pastries, fruit pies, crullers, donuts, and rice pudding.

The Olympia is a big-time operation. There are even two dishwashers. Like all true diners, the accent is on fast service. On weekends the clientele consists of big after-movie crowds, families, and travelers who opt for Routes 5 and 15 instead of the grind of the superhighway. John told us that when Interstate 91 was put in he lost 35 percent of his business.

The Olympia is a twenty-four-hour diner, and if you get a chance, stop by at night so you can admire the huge red neon sign that runs the length of the roof. The word *Olympia* is written out in bold script; next to that, in block letters, it says DINER. If you're lucky enough to pass by after a rainstorm, you'll see the sign reflected in the wet pavement of the parking lot.

# Curley's Diner

*Stamford, Connecticut*

Sometimes you find a diner owner who's bigger than his diner, bigger than life. Herluf Svenningsen, better known as Curley, is one of those people. Even though Curley, who's in his early seventies, has retired from the diner business, he's still strongly identified with the Stamford landmark that carries his name. When we called Curley's to get some background information on this 1949 Mountain View diner, the current owners, the Anastos family, said that we should set up an appointment and they'd have Curley on hand to give us the history.

The Anastos have tried hard to keep the original feel and appearance of the diner as intact as possible, and on the whole they have done a good job. The food is tasty and reasonably priced. Breakfast is a big meal there, especially on weekends. The diner still serves as the meeting place that Curley described to us. It's convenient to the highway, being visible from Interstate 95.

The rest of this piece belongs to Curley the man and his reminiscences, not only because he and his wife were kind enough to take us into their home and show us old photos and clippings, but because after all these years Curley still loves the diner world and is a member of a very select and slowly vanishing group of dinermen who helped create what diners are all about.

Curley is slightly surprised by what he calls the "obsession" that some people have with diners these days. He sees diners as a dying breed, being pushed into extinction by the massive advertising campaigns of the fast-food chains. But he still remembers a converted railroad car that sat on a siding in Omaha when he was a boy, and how workers would come there for lunch or a cup of coffee. It never occurred to him then that some day he'd be in the diner business.

Curley graduated from the Massachusetts School of Art in 1929, the year of the Big Crash. He went to New York, moved into the YMCA, and, quickly discovering that the Depression economy held little hope for an aspiring artist, took a job as a soda jerk. It was nearly fifty years before he stopped working behind the counter.

When Curley's Diner was brand-new, back in 1949, it was open twenty-four hours a day. Curley told us that the diner would be "inhabited by everything that walks or crawls at night." Bookies, cops, firemen, or streetwalkers—they'd all be there. Truck drivers too, or just plain insomniacs. The diner became a news network, and in the morning Curley would be able to find out everything that happened in town.

A world unto itself, Curley's Diner had its own life, and yet it played an important role in the community. Curley explained it this way: "The old-time diner was like a miniature city. You could get anything there. When the fire department or the utility workers were called out on an emergency, they would stop by and pick up tanks of coffee. You could almost always call here and get a cop, a doctor, or any type of information. It was like asking a neighbor for help." He also told us that if a customer had hit on hard times and was down and out, he could come into the diner and know he'd be fed. It was that type of place.

The stress was on being a part of the neighborhood. This is

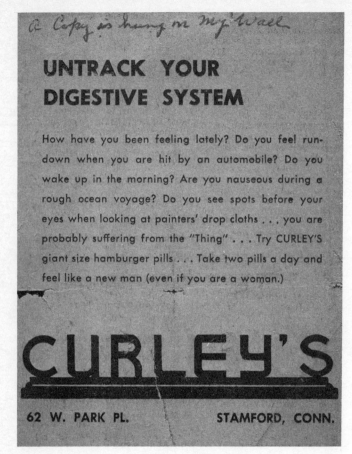

*Newspaper ad from Curley's Diner, circa 1950*

one of the things that bothers Curley about the fast-food restaurants today—no neighborhood contact. The old-time diner owner, he claims, knew his clientele and would know what they wanted to eat the minute they stepped through the door. He was friendly with everyone, and all his customers were treated as equals—and the way a customer is treated affects how a customer behaves.

There used to be a pinball machine in the diner. Every day at lunchtime, the president of the Stamford Trust, a local bank, and the manager of the Merrill-Lynch office in town would come in and play the machine to see who would pay for lunch. Not being the type to waste money, they'd use slugs. The diner was a place where they could relax and take a break from their professional roles. Today, if you walk into a McDonald's or a Burger King you stand on line, have maybe a minute's worth of contact with whoever's taking your order, and that's it. It's an isolating experience, compared to the personal contact you can have in a diner.

Besides having a lot to say about his customers, Curley talked quite a bit about the workers. It was from him that we first heard the expression "diner feet." Diner feet is a term that refers to the way a man who's put in more than a few years behind the counter walks. It comes from not having enough room to take full steps while working, so a counterman can develop a type of shuffle, or splayfoot walk. It's a unique way of walking, and anyone who's been afflicted with diner feet is marked for life as a diner worker. One night, while driving with some friends, we saw a fellow who had diner feet, and we felt just like Sherlock Holmes when we were able to identify his life's work.

In recalling the days when a cup of coffee was a nickel and a hamburger was a dime, Curley filled us in on how his countermen used to work. There were always three people behind the counter: a grillman, a middleman (who stood by the coffee urn), and a third man who worked the other end. They never crossed past one another—they couldn't, because there wasn't enough room. But they all had to work together, and they were dependent upon one another at all times. Because everything was done quickly and nothing was written down, the timing between the three of them had to be perfect. Being a good counterman is an exact science, and those who do it well take great pride in their work. It's not uncommon for a good grillman to speak about his teacher in a voice full of reverence, much the same way a spiritual disciple might refer to his holy master. This is no exaggeration. Working the grill is an art, a vernacular art created by the early diner owners.

All the workers were regarded as equal in importance by the diner owner, if not by each other. If a dishwasher failed to report to work, everything got fouled up. It then became the boss's job to wash dishes; the grillman or the waitress certainly wasn't about to do it. So sometimes Curley would find himself working more than his usual thirteen-hour day, but the long hours were worth it to this true dinerman who always found great pleasure in serving so many satisfied customers.

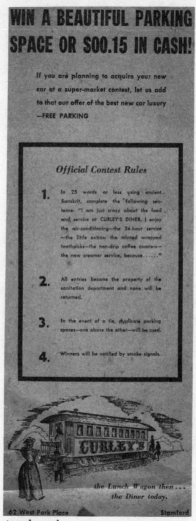

*Another ad*

## Skee's Diner

*Torrington, Connecticut*

*Skee's interior*

When we first saw Skee's Diner sitting by the Torrington traffic circle, we thought we had stepped into an early Popeye cartoon. Built in 1908 and moved here from its original site in Seymour, Connecticut, in 1945, the diner looks exactly as it did when it was first constructed by the Coachman Company over seventy years ago.

The current owners, Judy and Charlie Jacqueman, were born and raised in Torrington, and they have managed to maintain a feeling of warmth and a closeness to the community they serve. They bought Skee's in 1973, and with the building they also inherited all the original home-style recipes that we look for in a good diner. In addition, they have quite a few specials of their own.

Like all very early diners, Skee's has no separate kitchen. The cooking is done on the grill and the stove behind the black marble counter. There are no tables; the room is barely wide enough to accommodate the eighteen white-enameled stools. These stools sport brass footrests and, like everything else at Skee's, are in mint condition. The walls are mahogany, and the curved ceiling is tin. The sliding doors are mahogany and glass, and the old wooden icebox remains, having been electrified for modern use. All around the building are the same frosted Cambridge windows that were there in 1908, with the exception of one pane that was broken when a customer, jumping after having spilled hot coffee on himself, flung his briefcase through the glass.

Since the diner opens at 5:00 A.M., breakfast is a big meal at Skee's, and Judy and Charlie rise to the occasion. In addition to the fine bacon and eggs and hot cereals, there is a popular breakfast special called a "McGhee McMuffin." It is made from ham, egg, and cheese on a toasted muffin, it's a vast improvement over its fast-food namesake.

Skee's also serves a varied and quite reasonably priced selection of luncheon and dinner specials. There are two entrées a day, and these change daily. In the summer Judy and Charlie grow many of their own vegetables, and they never buy frozen meats. Everything is cooked with great care, with special attention given to the seasoning. For example, when preparing the Polish kielbasa with sauerkraut, Judy seasons the sauerkraut with bay leaves and raisins, according to an old family recipe, and then lets it simmer slowly for hours. It's delicious.

Tuesday night is Italian night at Skee's, and the same care goes into the seasoning of the spaghetti sauce, which also simmers for hours and leaves a pleasantly hot aftertaste. Other specials include roast turkey served with homemade bread stuffing, roast sirloin, which is sliced thin and served swimming in a rich brown gravy, and fried bologna with sauerkraut. The bologna is fried in batter right on the grill and served steaming hot with Judy's sauerkraut. All these platters come with bread and butter and a choice of two vegetables. Our one regret is that the whipped potatoes are made from a mix. Judy says she doesn't have the time or space to churn out the amount of potatoes the restaurant needs. Skee's is famous for its puddings which are cooked on the stove and sold for about 50 cents. They include grape nut, made from the cereal and cooked in a vanilla base, and bread pudding.

While we were eating the bread pudding, which is by far the best we've ever tasted, Judy talked about some of the regular customers she serves, many of whom have been coming to Skee's for over twenty years. There's the retired Mayor Daley of Torrington, who stops in every morning at 8:45 for his coffee and every afternoon at 1:15 for a glass of root beer. And the elderly gentleman who comes in for breakfast at the same time every morning, walks past the front door to the side entrance, and then will sit only on the fourth stool from the end. Judy cooks special meals for customers on restricted diets, and she likes to feel that her diner serves as a regular meeting place for members of the community. She fondly recalls the time when two of her patrons were accidentally reunited at her counter after not seeing each other for thirty years. Skee's offers the type of comfortable surroundings, with good food, that brings people closer together.

## Makris Diner

*Wethersfield, Connecticut*

*Mirrored pie case at Makris Diner*

Like its neighbor the Olympia, up the pike, the Makris Diner makes its own baked goods, and we think the pastries here may be the best we've had at any diner. Everything is baked from scratch by a seventy-eight-year-old baker who believes in doing things "the old way." By that, we mean he never cuts corners.

The inside of this 1951 O'Mahony is predominantly blue, and its stainless steel exterior is laced with brightly colored neon lights. Inside, the booths are blue. The counter has a blue top, and the blue base is broken by a broad yellow horizontal stripe. A mirror runs down the center of the ceiling, and the blue-tinted glass of the windows at the far end of the diner casts a blue hue throughout.

Steve McQueen once ate at this diner, when he was shooting a film nearby. He came without any cash and tried to pay for his spaghetti dinner with a credit card. The cashier just looked at him and told him this was a diner and didn't accept plastic. He was forced to call someone to pay his bill. The crowd that gathered while he was there became so huge that he was forced to eat in his car—one of the drawbacks of stardom. There is another story about a troupe of Mexican dancers who stopped at the Makris while on tour. They played a Greek selection on the jukebox and wound up dancing in the aisles. Such patrons are in sharp contrast to many of the regular customers, recently divorced single men who live in the many motels that are a part of the strip of fast-food restaurants, bowling alleys, and auto supply shops that make up this part of the Berlin Turnpike.

The Makris is a twenty-four-hour diner, closing only on Thanksgiving and Christmas Day. There are several Makris brothers, one of whom does all the cooking. They're very careful about the quality of the food and take the attitude that if they wouldn't want to eat it, they certainly won't serve it.

The prices are reasonable, and there are several specials daily. We had a cube steak sandwich, which was offered as a luncheon special with vegetable beef soup and coffee. We also tried the chicken pie and the baked sausages with brown gravy, potato, and vegetable. Everything was tasty, and the platters were large and filling.

The soups are all made from scratch, with Yankee bean, chicken vegetable, split pea, and tomato among those offered. Shrimp is still served, but lobster, once a favorite at the Makris, has become too costly for diner prices (most of the platters are priced between $2.50 and $3.50).

Among the baked goods, which are attractively displayed in a mirrored pie case behind the counter, are muffins (blueberry and corn), Danish, apple and fig squares, and pies. This is one of the very few diners we found that makes its own pie fillings and takes nothing out of a can. Because of the baker's age, we asked what would happen when he was no longer able to bake for them. The Makris brothers said they wouldn't be able to find another man who makes things the way he does so they would do the baking themselves.

As we said, the pastries at the Makris were the best we found anywhere. Some diners offered excellent pies or cakes, but when it comes to a full assortment of baked goods, the Makris is tops. And the coffee is great, too.

# Maine

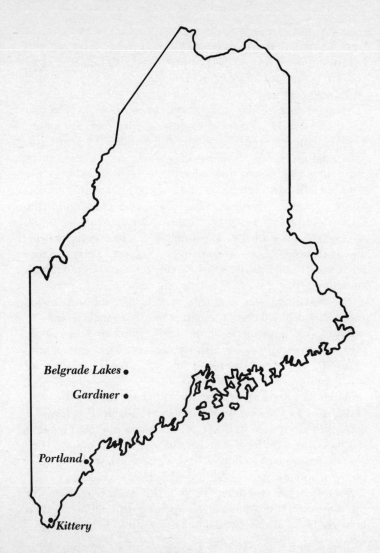

Belgrade Lakes •

Gardiner •

Portland •

Kittery

*Belgrade Lakes, Maine*

Old MacDonald's has the ambience of a diner, yet in visual appearance it can't be considered one. It defies categorization, yet it's unique and special enough that we have chosen to include it in this volume. Old MacDonald's is the creation of Terry MacDonald, who is both proprietor and cook. Terry had worked for twenty years in the diners, luncheonettes, saloons, fine restaurants, and bowling alley snack bars of New Jersey, and she was bored. She followed in the footsteps of her daughter Carolyn, who had moved north a year earlier, and in 1973 opened her own place.

The food served by Terry is all homemade, including the breads; practically the only thing that comes out of a can is the corn for the corn chowder. The food is so good that we wouldn't hesitate to drive an extra twenty miles out of our way to experience one of Terry's meals, even during a so-called gas shortage.

There are several different specials daily, and no menu is posted, so you'll have to ask Terry what's being offered each day. One thing that's always available is roast beef, which you can have as either a platter or a sandwich. It's cooked rare and is very tender. If you prefer your meat well-done, Terry will cut you a piece from the end of the roast. She serves the roast beef with her own gravy, which is prepared from meat drippings, flour, and the water that was used to cook the vegetables or potatoes. This vegetable water adds a tremen-

dous amount of flavor to the gravy, a secret Terry learned from her mom. The roast beef sandwich (which is made with homemade bread) is, in Terry's own words, "a monster." But she feels that it's more the tenderness than the size that appeals to people.

Sundays and Friday nights are the only times you can enter Old MacDonald's and be sure of what's on the menu. Friday night it's broiled scallops, and Sunday it's prime rib. The meat on Sunday is sliced very thick, costs about $6.00, and comes with potato and vegetable. Salad is 60 cents extra.

Other specials include sautéed chicken, which is almost always available. This is boneless breast of chicken sautéed in butter and lemon. Terry also makes a Russian vegetable pie, which contains cabbage, mushrooms, onions, cream cheese, and hard-boiled eggs, served in a pie crust. Terry decides what she'll make "as the spirit moves, or when people ask for something special."

The restaurant was forced to start baking its own breads when the local bakeries thought it was too much trouble to deliver. The homemade honey buns, blueberry and apple pies (made with local fresh fruits), chocolate cake, chocolate cake with a peanut butter icing, and cream pies are all excellent.

When we asked Terry how she felt about diners, she said, "Basically, I've always loved diners. Probably that's why I cook. We always ate in diners when we were growing up. If we had a choice where to eat, we'd go to a diner. They always have good coffee. They almost always have good pastries, and almost always they know how to cook eggs."

Before we left, we asked Terry if she had any message for the diner lovers of America. She paused for a moment, then her eyes lit up as she gave us her one-word answer: "Unite."

## Wakefield's Diner

*Gardiner, Maine*

Wakefield's is one of our favorite diners. A Worcester Lunch Car built in 1946, it's resplendent with its blue and black tiles and its lustrous mahogany. The food is all fresh and flavorful, and there's a warm, friendly feel to the place.

We met owner Albert Gibson in the kitchen, where he was ensuring quality control by carefully weighing out a portion of boiled dinner. Recently retired from his insurance business, Albert took over Wakefield's as a kind of hobby, something to keep him busy—and keep him busy it does, to the tune of about ten hours a day. But Albert loves it. He kept the same kitchen help that had been there for years, and the same waitresses, so the operation runs smoothly. He knows everyone in Gardiner from his business days, and he has the type of outgoing personality that helps create the neighborly feel the diner has.

One of the unusual features of Wakefield's is its location. Set right in the center of town, it's up against a bridge that runs over the Cobbeesee, a small river you can see from inside the diner if you sit at the end booth or stool. A foundation of thick steel girders holds the building up some forty feet above the river. The outside walls are painted a cream-colored enamel, and the monitor roof is strongly reminiscent of an old Pullman train car.

The inside of the diner is in gleaming condition. The counter top is a tan marble. The base of the counter and the walls along the six booths are tiled in blue and black. There is a wooden grill hood, and the window sashes are all oak. The barreled ceiling is a blue-marbled Formica, and each enameled panel is set in wood strips. Six small fluorescent lamps run the length of the ceiling, each with three short bulbs. The border along the ceiling, where it's recessed, is mahogany.

The booths are all made from mahogany, as is the side entrance, which is no longer used. There are many small touches in the design that add to the overall appearance of the diner: the way the cathedral-style window in the side door is cut, the work along the doorframe, the stainless steel sunbursts that adorn the wall behind the counter. The ceiling vents, which are opened by means of brass cranks set into the ceiling, are of stained glass. There are bright white letters in the black-faced sandwich boards, and a black-and-white-checked tile floor. The corners of the counters, where there's an opening between them to get to the grill, are made from curved glass bricks.

When we asked Albert what the small wooden cabinets above the icebox were for, one of his patrons quipped that they held the remains of the two previous owners. At any rate, you don't see such cabinets in every diner. They must have been one of the customized features offered by the Worcester Lunch Car Company.

The food at Wakefield's is all simple, fresh, and good. Sometimes you'll go into a town and find that it has its own little idiosyncrasy when it comes to seasoning food. In Gardiner it would appear to be vinegar. The boiled dinner, which is corned beef and cabbage, was served with a bottle of vinegar. Experimenting, we poured a little vinegar on the meat and found it to be an excellent complement. The boiled dinner, which was priced at less than $2.50, was served on a portioned plate with potatoes, carrots, and squash. We washed it down with a glass of refreshing pink lemonade. The coleslaw was homemade and slightly vinegary. Fresh-baked soda biscuits come with every meal.

Other platters include breaded pork or veal cutlets, American chop suey, fried haddock, scallops, and clam strips. One Wakefield's dish that you don't see too often is fried tripe. Albert told us it's mainly the old-timers who eat the tripe, a habit left over from Depression days. Every Friday there's baked stuffed whitefish, fresh from Boothbay Harbor, and, in months with an "r" in their names, oyster stew. Two of the most popular sandwiches at Wakefield's are the chicken salad sandwich and the lobster roll. For around $3.00 there is a rib roast plate that comes with potato, vegetable, dessert, and coffee.

Homemade donuts, plain and cinnamon, are displayed on the counter in old-fashioned donut jars.

Sitting in the corner booth, we were able to look out on the river and the old railroad station below. Across the street we saw a new driveway being laid at the Exxon station. Working without shirts, and wearing caps, the crew spread the tar and smoothed it out with a yellow steamroller. The open view from the diner creates a very light and airy feeling, which is another reason we enjoyed our stay at Wakefield's so much.

Below the diner there's a small apartment that Albert sometimes uses. It has a sundeck, where he's considering putting tables and serving customers. The sundeck offers a great view of the river. We thought that the apartment made the perfect spot to write a diner guidebook, and we fantasized about being able to work down there, with the best food in town being served right upstairs.

## Seagull Diner

*Kittery, Maine*

When Jimmy Canty first bought his diner from a cousin, twenty-five years ago, he didn't know the first thing about the business. He and his cousin didn't tell anyone the diner had been sold, and Jimmy went to work there as a dishwasher so he could quietly observe what was going on. One night, after he had been there two weeks, Jimmy suggested to someone that he pick up a broom and do some necessary sweeping. Well, that broke everyone up—the dishwasher telling another worker to sweep up. But Jimmy thought it was time to reveal his hand, since he had gotten a chance to see how each person worked and who was stealing what and how much (one waitress had actually asked him to help her carry out a bushel basket full of meat and vegetables). One of the workers called Jimmy's cousin, who informed them all that Jimmy was indeed the new owner. Needless to say, the workers went into shock, and some of them never came back to face their new boss.

Since that time, Jimmy Canty's place has prospered, becoming much more than a diner. A huge restaurant has been built on, and there are a bar and a disco downstairs. Although Jimmy still dresses simply—in jeans, work shirt, and boots—he has the air of a very wealthy man.

The Seagull Diner is a large stainless steel Worcester Lunch Car. It was the first such Worcester car we saw. The inside is mostly pink and green Formica, brightly lit with fluorescent lamps and kept very clean. The menu is quite extensive and not cheap. Anything served in the main dining room is available in the diner, which is the domain of Mama Jo.

Mama Jo has been waiting tables at the Seagull for twenty years, and everyone in the area knows her. For the past eight years she's been working the night shift at this twenty-four-hour diner. A no-nonsense woman, she tries her best to make everyone who comes into the diner feel right at home, and she does a good job. It's not for nothing that she's called Mama.

All the food served at the Seagull is fresh. The meats are even specially supplied by a neighboring farmer friend of Jimmy's. Jimmy claims to have the finest quality hamburger meat around, and he says the best hamburger comes from a fixed, or neutered, bull. The Seagull makes its own breakfast sausage, and they're the biggest we've ever seen. They look more like Italian sausage than something you'd find next to your eggs in the morning, and they are delicious. The whole pig is used, not just pork scraps, as is the case with some other sausages.

The breakfast menu is large and is one of the better buys for your dollar at this diner. Two eggs, with home fries and toast, cost about $1.60; ham, bacon, or sausage is another 60 cents. Blueberry muffins are made on the premises, and both pancakes and French toast are served. Something called a "Liz Omelet" is featured, made with peppers, onions, mushrooms, tomatoes, ham, and cheese.

Since the Seagull is located right by the water, there are plenty of fish dishes on the menu, all fresh. The fried clams are made from whole clams, belly and all, which provides a full flavor. Other fish dishes include baked stuffed haddock, fried shrimp, fried oysters, and finnan haddie. The fish prices run anywhere from slightly over $3.00 to $6.00 for a combination seafood plate. A lobster salad triple-decker club sandwich is also offered.

All the soups are made from scratch at the Seagull. Seafood chowder, lobster stew, and oyster stew are always on the menu (oysters only in season). There are vegetable, asparagus, and minestrone soups, among others.

The Seagull makes real mashed potatoes, as well as its own coleslaw, and the roast turkey comes from the whole bird— no turkey roll here. One dish served in the dining room you might want to try is the prime rib. Priced at $11.00, you get a full twenty-seven ounces of meat. Few people can eat it all at once.

The diner has a soda fountain and makes its own strawberry shortcake. Liquor is available, even at the counter.

Jimmy feels that he's in business to please the public. Great care is taken not only in the quality and the preparation of the food but also in seeing that the service is always excellent. Jimmy runs his business as if it's a family. Mama Jo has been with him for years, as has Ron, the restaurant manager. Together they form a powerful combination that is able to oversee a huge operation while never letting it become too impersonal.

We asked Jimmy if he ever had any thoughts about selling, and he scoffed at the idea. "The Lord spares me and the creek don't rise," he told us. "I'll be here." We're glad of it.

## Miss Portland Diner

*Portland, Maine*

We first heard of the Miss Portland Diner through the May 1949 issue of *Diner* magazine, a trade publication, serving diner owners. In that issue a feature section announced the openings of new diners. The Miss Portland is one of the few we read about that is still standing.

The original owners of the Miss Portland were a fellow named James Crowder, who had lost a leg in the great explosion in Portland Harbor during World War II, and Frank Venuti, brother to the late great jazz violinist, Joe Venuti. According to the *Diner* article, they had been friends and were reunited when stories of the explosion were carried in the nation's newspapers.

The diner was sold in 1968 to its present owner, Alex Karas. Alex has been in the restaurant business for forty-five years. An avid golfer as well as a terrific chef, Alex met his backer on the greens and was able to put up the cash to buy what is still, on the inside at least, a mint-condition Worcester Lunch Car. A transitional diner, it incorporates some stainless steel along with a lot of colored tiles (yellow, blue, black) and mahogany booths. There's also the light-tan marble counter that you see in so many Worcester cars.

Miss Portland opens at 5:00 A.M. and closes at 3:00 P.M., so its offerings are limited to breakfast and lunch. Most of the customers at the diner are regulars. There's a large federal office building next door, well as other local businesses, whose employees depend on the diner for their meals.

One of the specialties of the house is the clam stew. All the clams Alex serves are very fresh. He buys them from a husband-and-wife team that works out of the nearby Biddeford Pool. They come up with only four or five gallons a week, just the amount the diner needs, so Alex is their sole customer. The stew is simple and quite good. The clams are whole, bellies and all, which makes for a rich broth. The base of the stew is cream and butter. It's said to be the best in New England, and we've tasted none better. The stew goes for about $1.50 and, with bread and butter, is filling enough for a complete lunch.

Alex serves a free dessert with his entrées. He has a fresh pudding every day. Sometimes there's rice pudding, tapioca, or even an apple pandowdy—all homemade—but banana pudding is a standard on the menu and always available.

Friday is fish day at the Miss Portland. Alex fillets his own haddock and serves it baked and stuffed as a special. He tries to keep the price down, selling it for just over $2.00, and he makes a limited amount (forty servings). The reason for the limit is that when the platters sit out on the steam table, which is at 180 degrees Fahrenheit, they tend to shrink, and he likes to serve a big portion. Fried haddock is always available.

Everything is fresh at this diner. The Miss Portland makes its own coleslaw, potato salad, and fresh mashed potatoes. The soups, such as lentil, beef noodle, or fish stew, are all homemade. There used to be a big Jewish delicatessen in Portland, and when they closed, Alex picked up many of their customers with his hot pastrami and corned beef sandwiches and bagels and cream cheese.

Sitting in one of the diner's eighteen mahogany booths, we asked Alex how he felt about diners. He called them "a vanishing item on the American landscape." The difference between a diner and a restaurant, he said, is the price of the food and the speed of the service. "Turkey is turkey, scallops are scallops, and sirloin is sirloin. The difference is that a diner serves them at one half to one third the price of a restaurant."

Alex mentioned that there used to be ten or twelve diners in downtown Portland, and he feels that when the old train station was torn down and a lot of so-called urban renewal done, a large part of the city was destroyed. He mentioned some of the old diners that used to be nearby—the Union, the Winslow, and the Florist City. He then mentioned all the state senators and congressmen who've stopped in for a meal on their way up to the capital. He told us about the time the Miss Portland contestants all came in to eat breakfast, and how each one was wearing a ribbon with her name across her chest. And he told us a story about Bette Davis coming in late at night, back when the diner was open then.

We left feeling that we had made new friends of this beautiful diner and its owner, and we look forward to going back for lots more clam stew. When you go to the Miss Portland, be sure to check out a great little sign hammered onto a telephone pole that reads 3 LARGE EGGS/TOAST/HOME FRIES/$1.10. We thought it was a nice touch.

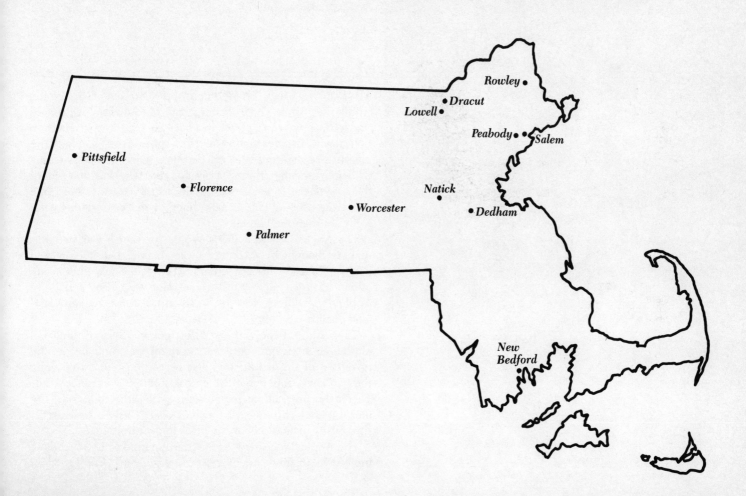

# Massachusetts

Rowley

•Dracut

Lowell•

Peabody
•Salem

Pittsfield•

Florence•

Natick
•

Worcester•

•Dedham

•Palmer

New
Bedford

## Apple Tree Diner

*Dedham, Massachusetts*

All that we knew of Dedham, prior to our visit to the wonderful Apple Tree Diner, had to do with Sacco and Vanzetti, so we were pleased to have two good experiences in that town. Besides eating at the Apple Tree, we had the pleasure of meeting Richard Gutman. Dick Gutman—along with John Baeder, the photo-realist painter—has done more than anyone else to document the history of the diner. We appreciated being able to talk diners with Dick and his wife, Kelly, in their new home.

The Apple Tree is a 1920s Worcester Lunch Car that was recently bought by a young couple, Joanne Dummeling and Warren Jones, who are diner lovers. They are purchasing other old lunch cars, with the intention of starting a chain of Apple Tree diners. It sure beats one of those modern fast-food chains.

The inside of the diner is all original. There's a long tan marble counter and, because the diner was built before the invention of the booth, two narrow counters that run along the windows, only one of which has stools so you can sit at it. The mahogany ceiling is polished daily with lemon oil. The nickel-plated chrome grill hood is also polished to a bright shine daily. The tile floor is a black and white mosaic.

The Apple Tree's new owners have added some touches of their own to give the diner an antique feel. For instance, there are green chandeliers hanging from the barreled ceiling, and lots of old pictures and magazine ads decorate the place. There's a strong apple motif that runs through the decorations. The saying "An apple is a tree expressing itself," hangs on one wall. There are also many pictures that include the image of an apple in them.

The outside of the diner is painted bright red. APPLE TREE DINER is painted on the exterior wall in bold letters. The monitor roof makes this lunch car look like a converted trolley car, which it's not.

Joanne and Warren have a sense of the diner's traditional role in the community, and they enjoy being involved with their customers. At Christmastime, Warren dresses up like Santa and waves hello to all who drive by. There are apples on the counter in the fall, and cookies for the Christmas season. During one recent winter, a blizzard left many people stranded, they were able to find food and shelter at the Apple Tree.

All the food is prepared fresh. Items that cannot be prepared on the grill are cooked in the kitchen of the house out back. There is no kitchen in the diner itself.

Breakfast is a big meal here. Joanne told us that she's all alone behind the counter from 6:00 A.M. to 7:00 A.M., and she called that time the "dirty hour." It's all men inside, eating their breakfast on the way to work. For that one hour each day, the diner reverts to the era when it was a place for men only. She says the men are great, and she enjoys being the only woman around them.

Two eggs with toast cost 95 cents. Two eggs with home fries were $1.25. Of course, these prices are subject to change. Two eggs, sausage, toast, and home fries were priced at $1.80 when we were there. Coffee, advertised as a bottom-

less cup, is 40 cents. Steak and eggs, and corned beef hash and eggs, are also available, as are pancakes and French toast. There's a full selection of omelettes. Possible ingredients appear on the menu under the heading "Make Your Own."

Plenty of sandwiches and several different types of burgers are listed, and there are different specials daily. The day we were there, the special was meat loaf. Each meat loaf was prepared as an individual serving and shaped like a small football. It was very good, flavored with a touch of vinegar and brown sugar, as well as other seasonings.

The Apple Tree is famous for its baked goods, which are supplied by a local baker who uses only fresh ingredients. There is, of course, apple pie, as well as cinnamon bread, chocolate éclairs, a pinwheel cheese cake, and special holiday cakes. Because we were there in the springtime, we saw the Italian Easter bread.

The menu at the Apple Tree is decorated with a drawing of the diner and an apple tree on the front. The back cover gives a brief history of the development of diners, and inside there is a paragraph telling the patron a little something about the history of this particular diner.

We enjoyed our visit to the Apple Tree. The owners have managed to maintain the original diner feel while adding a few decorative touches of their own. We were reminded of other diners, most notably the Empire in New York City, where a sense of modern slickness has destroyed the old diner qualities. Joanne and Warren have managed to avoid that in their mixing of the past and the present.

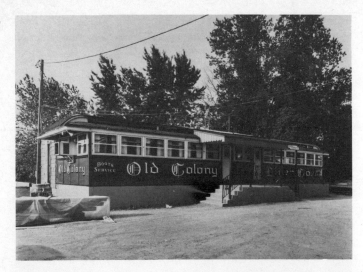

*The impressive Leo Dalphond*

## *Old Colony Diner*

*Dracut, Massachusetts*

We first heard of the Old Colony from a dinerman in Peabody who remembered this lunch cart from its earlier incarnation in Dorchester. His aunt used to own it when it was there, and he spent much of his youth working behind the counter. That was thirty-five years ago. He suggested that we try to locate it if we could, as it was a real beauty.

Well, he was right; it's still around, and it *is* a beauty. Standing right along the Merrimac River in a small town north of Lowell, it's a sixty-foot-long, bright-red-enamel Worcester Lunch Car. It's so long we thought it might be two diners joined together, but owner Leo Dalphond took us down to the basement and showed us the solid steel beams, forming part of the building's foundation, that attest to its original construction.

Leo is planning to add a dining room and lounge to the existing structure. This addition, which is to look like a deckhouse and offer a fine view of the river, would be open only at night and would not interfere with the diner's operation or appearance. We're glad to hear that, as this is practically a mint condition Worcester Car, and we would hate to see it ruined.

Leo has only owned this diner since the middle of 1976. His income comes mainly from his oil business in town, and the Old Colony is really a hobby for him. He's well known locally and obviously enjoys entertaining his friends in the warm environment of his lunch wagon.

The food at the Old Colony is simple, fresh, and well prepared. Because many people in Dracut are of French-Canadian descent, baked beans are a popular item on the breakfast menu, and the baked beans are homemade here. Prepared from California pea beans, they're made "French style"—that is, baked with salt pork but no molasses—and they are good. There are different specials daily, and Leo does some catering. Saturday is the slow day at the Old Colony, and the menu is limited to mostly burgers and franks and beans, but you might be lucky enough to sample the meat loaf, and there are always fresh baked goods.

Salmon pie is one of the house specialties, as is pork pie. They are both cooked in a regular pie crust and served sliced into individual portions. The fish is covered with a cream sauce, and the pork a red gravy, both homemade. The pies are offered with a side of mashed potatoes (instant) and are very reasonably priced. Another special is the stuffed cabbage, made with rice, hamburger, onions, and seasonings. The meat loaf is baked with bacon strips on top, which not only gives the meat extra flavor but prevents it from drying out.

Something that we were not familiar with are pork scraps. A simple dish, pork scraps are really ground pork meat, sautéed with onions. They're a local favorite.

All the soups at this diner are prepared from scratch. Tomato, vegetable, and pea soups and a fish chowder are some of the selections.

Although there have been some changes inside the diner, most notably the addition of a bar, there is enough of the original left to delight us. Part of the clear glass counter top is still intact, and we were able to sit there and see all the fresh baked goods displayed beneath the glass. Apple pies, apple and lemon turnovers, and breakfast muffins all looked tempting, and they tasted as good as they looked.

Outside the diner, there is a broad canopy over the center entranceway. The diner's name is painted in bright yellow Gothic script against the red enamel siding. Inside there is a lot of wood: The barreled roof, the booths, and the walls are all made of oak and mahogany. The old wooden icebox was replaced long ago with an identical white porcelain replica. There are large ivory tiles along the base of the counter, and the molding around the glass counter top, once brass-plated, is now worn down to its original steel.

The green stools have squared-off white porcelain bases, and a brass footrest runs the length of the counter. The floor is completely tiled in green. We felt very comfortable eating there, and it was apparent that the other customers felt right at home.

This is another diner with limited hours, but it's worth coming in for breakfast or lunch. Or both. Be sure to say hello to Leo; everyone does.

*Florence, Massachusetts*

===============

For months after we first hit the diner trail, people kept insisting that we stop at the Miss Florence. No matter where they came from, everybody seemed to know about it. One woman told us how she would drive far out of her way just to eat the breakfast muffins. We're not sure why it's so famous. We did have a pretty good meal there, but it was nothing spectacular. Maybe it's the atmosphere; when you're inside, it *feels* like a great diner.

The Miss Florence was built during the 1930s by the Worcester Lunch Car people. The present owners, the Alexander family, took it over in 1941. They moved it across the street to its present location, digging a new cellar with a team of workhorses. We spoke with one of the owner's sons, Tommy, who grew up working in the diner and now manages it while he works toward a degree in pharmacology. Like many children of old-time diner owners, Tommy speaks with some bitterness about the long hours his father had to put in to keep the business going. He values the experience of working in the diner, learning how to deal with the people and the job, but there is an undercurrent of displeasure about the fact that if he wanted to see his father he'd have to look for him behind the counter.

The Miss Florence is no longer just a diner—a bar and a dining room have been added—but the diner is still the heart of the operation. We heard talk that the place was up for sale, so there might be some changes made, but we imagine it will remain basically the same.

Except for the early morning, when the booths and counter are filled with customers who've stopped for breakfast on their way to work, this is essentially a college diner. The Miss Flo is near to Smith College, Amherst College, and the University of Massachusetts. Tommy told us that the early morning clientele come in predictable shifts. At 6:00 A.M. there are the independent workers, roofers, masons, and the self-employed; at 7:30, the blue-collar workers; at 8:15 and 8:30, the white-collar workers; and between 9:00 and 10:00 the doctors, lawyers, and professional people, as well as some students and many of the same people who were in earlier, coming back for their coffee breaks. That's when the classic diner moment occurs—a lawyer and a junkyard owner sitting side by side. This is what makes Tommy call the diner "a United Nations with a knife and fork."

Because they have a regular restaurant and a full-sized kitchen, the menu at the Miss Florence is quite extensive, and too large to list even half the things served. Liquor is available. Most of their soups are homemade, and if they come out of a can something is always added. There is an excellent clam chowder, New England-style, and lobster, oyster, clam and scallop stews. Also on the menu are barbecued spareribs with the diner's own sauce, roast duckling, and roast stuffed Rock Cornish game hen. There's even chicken chow mein with Chinese noodles.

Of the long list of seafood, some is fresh and some is frozen. Check with your waitress to see which selections are fresh. Baked stuffed scallops, fried fillet of haddock, broiled swordfish, salmon, brook trout, and scrod are but a few of the selections. There are several lobster dishes, buttered lobster en casserole, breaded lobster squares with drawn butter, and lobster salad. You could also have a clam roll or even a fried oyster sandwich.

The homemade coleslaw is delicious. Lox and bagel is just one of the many sandwiches offered. The french fries are like potato puffs and look more interesting than they taste.

Tommy told us that, in the face of this enormous selection of foods, the favorite in the diner is still the meat loaf and the pan-browned corned beef hash and egg.

All the pies are baked on the premises. For the most part, canned fillings are used, but fresh fruits are added when in season. There's blueberry, pecan, and squash pie. Several cream pies—pineapple, lemon, banana, chocolate, and coconut—are always available. Among the homemade puddings, we particularly liked the Indian pudding, which is made from cornmeal, eggs, sugar, nutmeg, and molasses. You don't run across it too often, and it's a real treat.

There have been some changes made in the interior of this diner. It's been lengthened, and the marble counter has been replaced with Formica. Too many plates were breaking against the hard marble, which Tommy called "unforgiving."

Everyone who was inside the Miss Florence seemed to be very aware of the fact that they were in a diner. Even the waitress, a young student, told us that her name was "Pat Hurley, a real diner name," and she had only been working there for two weeks. Maybe that's what bothered us, that people were too self-conscious about the Miss Florence being a diner. Tommy complained about it a little himself. At any rate, we liked him, and we enjoyed our stay at his diner. Even if we are a little ambivalent, we recommend that you check it out yourself.

*Lowell, Massachusetts*

We had an instand rapport with Daphne Zoukis, the owner's daughter, at the Owl Diner. Daphne is a graduate student, and at one point she traveled to the mills of nearby Lynn to record an oral history of the lives of the older millworkers. So, unlike some diner owners, she understood immediately what we were doing, traveling from diner to diner with our tape recorder, attempting to make a record of a vanishing fixture of twentieth-century America.

The Owl is an old Worcester Lunch Car; they claim that it's at least forty-five years old but were not sure of its exact age. At any rate, it's easy to see that it was once a real beauty, although time has worn it down somewhat.

The color scheme inside, in addition to the abundance of woodwork, is mostly an orange-red and black. The counter top is black marble, and the base is red tile with a black stripe. The refrigerator, built against the wall behind the counter, is red porcelain. The grill hood is stainless steel, and the booths and stools are upholstered in black.

As we rode toward the Owl, we asked ourselves if we might discover the diner where Jack Kerouac used to eat. We should have had a clue when we were told that the Owl is situated alongside of the old railroad terminal, but our suspicions weren't aroused until we saw the faces of the men at the counter. We were talking to Daphne and her friend Tim about the old grillman at the Owl. They were telling us of his amazing ability to remember twenty orders at once and keep them all going on the grill. While they raved about his speed, they tried to remember his name. "Was it Jerry?" Daphne asked, "Jerry LeBlanc?" Suddenly a voice called over to us from the counter, "LeBranch. Jerry LeBranch." We looked over to see who had offered the information and were startled to see the stark French-Canadian features of a young man who, dressed in a baggy sports coat, could easily have stepped from a dust-jacket photo for *On the Road*. So we asked Daphne if Kerouac had ever eaten there, and she told us a sad story about the great writer.

Nick, Daphne's dad, went to school with Jack Kerouac, and they played together on the same football team. So he used to eat at the diner quite a bit, especially in his later years. Most of the customers at the Owl are veterans of World War II, and they live in the houses that line the avenue on which the diner is situated. Existing on disability payments, they spend many hours seated at the counter over a cup of coffee. To them, the man we know as the father of the Beat Generation was nothing more than a drunken bum. They had chided him constantly, telling him that he was washed up, that he'd never write anything worthwhile. Nick had helped him out, but Daphne says that it was pathetic to hear about the way he was treated.

The food at the Owl is your basic diner food, and it's all well prepared. Eggs and omelettes are the biggest sellers, and there's a large selection of steaks and chops. They make their own baked beans, using Gravy Master, ketchup, pork, and sugar with their pea beans. All the soups are also made from scratch.

The prices are reasonable, but, like many New England diners, there is an extra charge for home fries with your eggs, and a charge for a second cup of coffee.

A dining room has been added to the diner, which is open late Tuesday, Friday, and Saturday nights. Daphne's mom painted the walls herself, filling them with murals depicting undersea scenes.

In addition to many regular everyday customers, the Owl gets its share of the strange ones. There's Carmen, a local transvestite, who has become a fixture over the years. And there's a university professor whose mind is not quite what it used to be. Instead of teaching advanced calculus, he now dresses up as Dracula and sips his coffee in a flowing black cape.

Our experience at the Owl diner got us thinking about how the diner seems to function in some way as an archetypical symbol that affects people on a basic subconscious level. For the many months before, during, and even after the writing of this book, diners appeared in our dreams nightly. Our editor even told us, after reading most of the manuscript, that he too dreamed of diners. We don't know what it is that attracts people. Eddy, the guy who was the Kerouac look-alike, told us that "you get every type of person who's walking the earth" in the Owl Diner. Other diner workers have told us the same thing. Somehow the lunch wagon serves as a common denominator. We can't pinpoint why, but if you have any ideas on the subject, please let us know.

At any rate, don't miss the owl-shaped neon sign outside this diner.

## Casey's Diner

*Natick, Massachusetts*

*Casey's Diner*

At last, a diner that someone had enough sense to designate a state landmark. Casey's Diner is a fifty-five-year-old Worcester Lunch Car, the type that was referred to as a "dog wagon" in the old days. With only ten stools and a window for takeouts, Casey's manages to go through four hundred franks a day.

This tiny bungalow of a diner has been in Natick, and owned by the Casey family, since 1925. Joe Casey, a soft-spoken fellow in his early fifties, has run it with his wife since 1958, when he took it over from his father. Before the elder Casey had bought the current lunch car, he owned a horse-drawn lunch wagon. That was back in 1885, and the wagon was a small affair, with a mere four stools. Every day at 3:00 P.M. he'd draw the wagon into the park in the center of town, where it would sit until 1:00 A.M., when he'd return it to the barn until the following day. Because the wagon was so small, most people would sit in the park and eat their hot dogs. We were told that, later on, the wagon was sold to gypsies who took it up to Maine.

Casey's used to be open twenty-four hours a day, but now there's no movie theater in Natick and people just stay home watching TV and eating Ritz crackers. With no nightlife, no one goes out for a late-night snack, so the diner has trimmed its night time hours.

*Joe Casey*

58

*Lunchtime at Casey's*

Joe was out when we got to the diner, so we waited for him in the kitchen with Mrs. Casey. She showed us snapshots of the recent moving of the diner from its original spot to its current location. It took twelve minutes to move the place a few blocks, and it cost about one hundred dollars a minute. The move made the local headlines.

When Joe walked into the kitchen, he was greeted with the news that somebody had just ordered twenty-five dogs to go, not an uncommon occurrence. Dogs are the specialty of the house, and they're cooked in gleaming copper pots that are made exclusively for Casey's. There are no soups or platters at this diner, just burgers, sandwiches, and hot dogs. On Fridays, fried fish-cake sandwiches are served for 50 cents.

Casey's hot dogs are served steamed—that is, the rolls are steamed soft and warm before they are filled with the hot dog, onion, mustard, and relish (called a "dog all around"). The hot dog rolls are prepared in a special copper steamer, a pot that looks like a bucket. Rows of rolls are placed in a perforated copper tray that is set into the pot above a few inches of boiling water. The water level is controlled by pouring the liquid into the kettle through a spout on its side.

The inside of Casey's is all oak, including the counter, which shows grooves formed by the wear of countless elbows. The center of the ceiling is recessed, and there are two small window vents inside the recessed portion. The walls are lined with old photos, including several shots of huge testimonial dinners from the town's past. There is also a shot of Joe's dad standing beside his horse-drawn wagon. The highly polished chrome hood is made from Monel, the special nickel alloy which, as noted in the Introduction, was developed in Germany and became the rage in diner technology during the 1920s. It maintains its high sheen to this day. The coffee is made in an old-fashioned urn, where the hot water is poured over the beans. Even the handles of the gas valves at the small grill are the original porcelain. The only change made was the replacing of the wooden tonic chest, which used ice. When Joe took the place over, he called the Worcester Lunch Car people to have an electric tonic chest put in. The same man who had built Casey's thirty-three years earlier showed up to do the installation and was amazed at the mint condition of the diner.

Casey says that the secret of running a good dog wagon is good food—and "move those stools." At lunchtime people are lined up inside, waiting for a stool to be free so they can sit down to eat. Some people have ketchup on their dogs, and occasionally some kid'll ask for mayonnaise, but however they're served, they are the best in New England. The lines are long at the side window, and every once in a while there'll be a contest to see who can eat the most. The record stands at eighteen in one sitting.

Pies are served at Casey's, so stop in for a cup of coffee and a slice of Table Top. But once you see those gleaming copper kettles, we dare you to resist. If only we could still get dogs like this at the ball park!

## Orchid Diner

*New Bedford, Massachusetts*

The message on the menu at Gabe Moura's Orchid Diner says that this is "The Place with the Friendly Atmosphere," and that's no lie. Gabe is one of the all-time great diner personalities. He's the only diner owner we ever interviewed in his own home while he was wearing a robe and pajamas. Nursing a cold, Gabe was still willing to tell us his philosophy about running a diner. It's hard work, and the pressure forced him to have a heart valve bypass operation. He gladly showed us the scar, à la Lyndon Johnson.

New Bedford has many people of Portuguese descent, and a number of dishes on the menu of this 1951 O'Mahony diner reflect the town's makeup. But this is not a Portuguese diner, and it specializes in high-quality diner fare.

Gabe has very definite feelings about what is a diner and what isn't. His definition is very simple: "If you can't move it, as far as I'm concerned, it's not a diner." He has as little use for the modern so-called diner as we do. He even feels that all the noise—the hustle and bustle behind the counter—is part of what makes a true diner.

Gabe likes everything up front, and by that we mean more than the grill. He's not afraid to say what he thinks, and he claims that insulting the customer is an art, that if it's done right, nobody feels hurt. He told us about one fellow who kept harassing him over the way his eggs were served. Gabe said, "Five dollars' worth of service, ten dollars' worth of aggravation, for a buck-and-a-half plate of eggs. Who needs it? Get out, because I'm the food boss. If you're successful, people say you're lucky. If you fail, they'll call you a jerk. So there's only one person you have to please—yourself. If you serve quality and cleanliness, I say you don't have to romance the customers."

The food at the Orchid is simple, well prepared, and served quickly. A big part of the diner business is getting patrons in and out fast. The prices are reasonable: a full dinner costs about $3.00.

Different specials are available daily. Beef stew was one of the dishes we tried, and it was excellent. There are sandwich specials, such as chicken salad roll with french fries and homemade coleslaw, which was selling for $1.75. Other offerings include chicken croquettes, shepherd's pie, ham and spinach with boiled potato, and breaded veal cutlets. On the menu one day we were there was kale soup made with *linguica* (a Portuguese sausage), *charissa*, kidney beans, and pork hocks; it had a spicy taste that we enjoyed.

Lately, Gabe's been running a series of radio ads which has all New Bedford talking. They're called "Love of Lunch" and are done in the style of a soap opera, complete with quaking organ music. One of them goes something like this: "The Love of Lunch, being brought to you by Gabe Moura's Orchid Diner. Since we left you last week, Gabe's son-in-law has been doing quite well. He's learned to make French toast, and bacon and eggs, but seems to have misplaced the recipe for ice cubes during a mysterious encounter with Bob Anderson, an early morning regular. And now, Lillian, the night counterwoman, has just gotten a promotion. She is

manager of the ladies' room." The disc jockey also plays a version of "Name That Tune," with the winner getting a free muffin at the diner.

We were fortunate enough to meet Gabe's wife, who told us that his mind is always at the diner. Once, when they were on vacation in Pennsylvania, Gabe got up at five in the morning and helped out at the motel restaurant. He had to keep calling the diner when they were vacationing in Hawaii. Gabe responded by saying that a diner owner must have an understanding wife, because of the long hours and total involvement required.

Gabe is also very involved with the New Bedford community. He helped set up a program in town for kids with learning disabilities, a program that evolved from the things he has learned in the diner business about working with people.

There are two other diners in New Bedford, but nowhere is there a diner like the Orchid, or another dinerman like Gabe Moura.

*Palmer, Massachusetts*

The Day And Night is one of the few diners we found that's run only by women. It was bought from the previous owner by his daughter, Tina Siock (pronounced "shook"). The head chef is a woman, and the waitresses behind the counter work the grill. The food has been prepared fresh in this Worcester Lunch Car since it was built in 1944, and the customers would stop coming in if anything were ever changed.

Palmer is a town that stopped growing fifteen years ago when the main industry moved out. Most of the people who eat at the Day And Night are middle-aged or older and have been coming in for a long time. They like their food "home-cooked," their portions big, and their prices small. Tina does her best to preserve this tradition.

We heard stories about the shows that used to go on behind the counter in the town's heyday, before everything closed up at three o'clock in the afternoon as it does today. One of the waitresses, Helen, told us that back when her brother Jimmy owned the Day And Night, regular weekday customers would bring their kids in on Saturdays to be entertained. Jimmy would make the eggs and pancakes do acrobatics over the grill by flipping them high in the air and then catching them behind his back. The kids would go crazy when they saw this. There was another waitress, Judy, who used to work there, and she'd ask the kids how they would like their pancakes to look, "Like a chicken or a duck?" Then she'd pour the batter on the grill in the shape of the animal, and the kids would really go wild. Of course they'd ask Dad to bring them back the following Saturday.

All the food in the kitchen is prepared by Tina and the head chef, Donna. Donna lives in a carriage house on a nearby estate, and she is occasionally hired by the estate owners to prepare elegant dinner parties. Some of the guests she's served include Arthur Fiedler and Dick Cavett, and she'll be cooking for a week before she's made all she needs for one of these meals. So Donna is an expert in the kitchen, and even though the regular customers like their food simple, she always sees to it that it tastes good.

The Day And Night serves a breakfast special that's hard to beat: two eggs, toast, coffee, and home fries for 99 cents plus tax. Pancakes and coffee go for the same price in the mornings. The luncheon special is called a businessman's special. It's a sandwich made from the meat of the day, a cup of soup, potato chips, and a beverage for just under $2.00. A different roast is prepared in the oven each day; the day we were there it was boned pork roast.

Two fresh vegetables are served daily. In the winter one is usually carrots, but in the warm weather the selection extends to whatever is fresh and available. Day And Night makes its own coleslaw, grating the cabbage by hand, and pickles its own beets (using sugar, grated onion, garlic powder, and Italian dressing, along with a few secret touches). Fresh turnips are also a favorite vegetable year-round, along with broccoli and cauliflower.

The Day And Night has a lobster salad roll, french fries, and coleslaw combination for just over $2.00, and the hamburg special, which is a hamburger on a bun with lettuce, tomato, and mayonnaise, is 80 cents.

The kitchen is small, but the limited space is used well. We saw what looked like a pudding sitting on top of the stove and found out it was a cross between a pudding and a cake, called "Nobby Apple Pie." Made almost like apple cake, it's served hot, with whipped cream or ice cream. Other desserts include cherry cobbler, apple brown Betty, bread pudding, and tapioca. Dessert prices run about 65 cents. The diner bakes its own breakfast muffins.

Helen told us that most of the toll booth operators on the turnpike come from Palmer, so that whenever travelers ask where they can get off the highway for a good meal, it's always the Day And Night that's recommended. Helen also told us that sometimes after she's gone home from work she laughs all night thinking about some of the things that have gone on during the day. "Maybe you'll think this is gross," she told us, "but these girls used to come over from the bank every day, and, um, we were real busy and I'm running around like crazy, you know, and I go over and ask one girl, 'What are you going to have?' And the soup that day was pea soup. So she asks for a bowl. So I turn around and shout, 'A bowl of pea,' and the whole diner breaks up."

*Peabody, Massachusetts*

If you visit the Red Rambler in Peabody, be sure to try the steak and eggs. The Goodmans, a husband-and-wife team who run this diner, marinate the steak in a vinegar and oregano base (we thought we tasted some Worcestershire sauce in there), and then grill it "Texas style" on an open flame. The flames sear all the juices and flavor in, and the result is delicious. Served with home fries and coffee, the whole thing costs about $2.50. We noticed one heavily tattooed customer sitting at a table eating it, and when we asked how he was enjoying his meal, his reply was most enthusiastic.

All food at this old Worcester Lunch Car is top quality. Everything is made from scratch, and the Goodmans, who also run a diet workshop, are well aware of the value of fresh foods. They've been in the diner business for only a few years, and they seem to enjoy what they're doing. Most of their customers are locals, regulars, and, as in many other towns, the diner serves as a social gathering place for people who live and work in Peabody.

The Red Rambler looks just like its name suggests. Painted bright red outside, with its name in white letters, and a black shingled roof, it may appear slightly ramshackle but is far from run down. The inside is kept spotlessly clean, with the barreled ceiling painted a light blue and the walls around the windows and the wooden cabinets under the grill painted pink. There's white tile under the counter and windows, with a black mosaic geometric pattern inlaid. The floor is a beautiful black-and-white tile mosaic. The bases of the stools along the counter are squared-off white enamel, braced against a brass footrest that runs the length of the counter.

A small addition has been made to the diner, allowing a few extra tables. White lace curtains with a red trim decorate the windows by the booths. One of the original windows, with its etched glass, is still visible at one end of the diner. The whole place is very homey. Just looking at it, you'd expect good home cooking, and you'd be right.

The Goodmans offer different specials daily. Monday and Tuesday are always potluck days. You might find baked macaroni and cheese or fresh brisket or pot roast on these days: whatever's available, and whatever Mrs. Goodman feels like cooking. Wednesday is Italian day. They might serve their baked lasagna, or veal cutlet with pasta, or the stuffed shells, made with plenty of mozzarella. Thursday is traditionally the day for boiled dinner in this part of the world, corned beef and cabbage. Friday is fish day, of course. In addition to the fine fish chowder with huge chunks of codfish floating in it, there's baked haddock, in a special creole sauce, and stuffed scallops. The scallops are placed on a layer of Ritz cracker crumbs, coated with another layer and seasoning, and then baked in the oven. This is a Red Rambler specialty and is out of this world.

We mentioned that the Goodmans run a diet workshop, but it is in no way connected with their diner. Many customers notice the large amount of weight they've lost and ask what it is that they eat. The answer is "mostly salads," and the Goodmans do serve a diet salad, which is tossed greens with turkey breast or dry tuna added.

All soups are made from scratch; a delicious Jewish-style sweet cabbage soup, a meatball lentil soup, as well as chicken rice and chicken gumbo are offered.

Fresh bagels are available daily; they arrive still warm from a local bakery. Your sandwich is served on dark rye if you request it. All sandwiches are very thick. The Goodmans make their own corned beef; their pastrami comes from a special source and is top quality.

The only thing that we didn't understand about the Red Rambler is the coffee. Not that there's anything wrong with the coffee per se, but they serve it in Styrofoam cups. Why? We don't know. But it seems that if they're going to put so much care into everything else, they could at least give you a real cup and saucer.

Peabody is a leather-goods town. If you go there, you might want to stop off at some of the outlet stores and look for a decent buy on a jacket, coat, or even a pair of pants.

*Pittsfield, Massachusetts*

Adrienne's Diner is another diner that enjoyed a previous life elsewhere. In this case it was Albany, New York, where Nelson Rockefeller is reported to have enjoyed a good diner meal while he was governor. We should alert diner purists that some changes have been made inside—you might say the place has been "customized"—but nothing has been done to change its flavor as a diner. Most noticeable are the new booths and the very low new stools, reminiscent of a 1950s lunch counter at a Woolworth's or a Rexall Drugs. A dining room has been added on downstairs and is available for parties. The barreled ceiling is still intact, and blue neon lights, part of the original diner, illuminate the booths.

Adrienne's is owned by Adrienne Chalifoux, who spends most of his time repairing automobiles while his wife, Carolyn, turns out delicious home-cooked meals. Their daughter, Anna, also helps out by waiting on tables.

Pittsfield is in the heart of the Berkshires. The area is full of summer homes, camps, beautiful resorts, and Tanglewood, famous for its concert series. After 10:00 P.M. everything else in Berkshire County closes up, and Adrienne's is about the only place to go for a late-night snack. You can see many of the musicians from Tanglewood relaxing over a midnight breakfast after a hectic concert schedule.

Breakfast is the big event at this diner. In the summer, when the town is full of displaced New Yorkers, customers are known to wait on line half an hour for a booth. Why? you may ask. It could be that waiting on line makes these city-dwellers feel right at home, but more likely it's the superior quality of all the food that's served at Adrienne's.

The eggs are local—farm-fresh—and the sausage links are as thick as knockwurst and made without preservatives (the ingredients are listed right on the menu). The home fries are made from a secret recipe, and we found them to be unadorned but basically honest. Two eggs with sausage and home fries do not come cheap—they'll run you about $3.00—but we think it's well worth it. Two eggs with toast and coffee cost $1.45; home fries are an additional 65 cents. A cheese omelette with toast and coffee costs about $2.00, and cold cereal is 65 cents.

Two specials of the house are the spaghetti sauce and the homemade soup. The sauce simmers for at least six hours each day, so you can't go wrong with the pasta. The hot sausage and spaghetti costs about $3.00; the chicken with spaghetti is priced slightly higher. No one knows what goes into the soup; it's another of the secret recipes. The soup isn't even listed on the menu, so you have to request it. We will say that it's thick and very delicious.

The french fries are homemade, from real potatoes, and we could count on the fingers of one hand the number of diners we found that have real french fries. They're sliced thin, and a large plateful costs $1.75.

In the summertime, all the vegetables served are fresh. Usually the selection includes asparagus, several types of squash, and turnips.

Carolyn cooks for the diner the same way she's cooked for her family for years. There's a wholesome sense of family inside this restaurant, a sense of integrity that carries over into the way the food is prepared and served. We found it very comfortable.

On the menu is the classic message: "Welcome to Adrienne's. If we please you, tell your friends, if not, please tell the management." We felt this is one place where they really mean it.

## Agawam Diner

*Rowley, Massachusetts*

The Agawam Diner in Rowley, Massachusetts, is really the Agawam number two. It's a stainless steel Fodero diner, built in 1954. The Agawam number one, which was in Ipswich, Massachusetts, was a bright-red Worcester Lunch Car built in 1941. There's a model of the old Agawam set in a frame over the door to the kitchen. The manufacturer used it as a showcase in magazine ads, and it can still be seen today in Newburyport, Massachusetts going under the name of the Fish Tail. It's worth the trip.

The Agawam was jumping when we pulled in on a rainy Saturday morning. It seemed as if the whole town had stopped in for breakfast: young people in jeans, hunters in flannels, the horsey set in boots and jodhpurs. We even saw the Bob Seger rock band, which must have been on tour.

The specialty at the Agawam is the baked goods, but the diner is also known for its seafood. Everything served is prepared on the premises, according to Smiley Galanes, one of the owners.

The Agawam is a family business started by four brothers and one brother-in-law back in 1941. The baker, Jimmy, who's been there since 1954, is a nephew. Family pride goes into everything the diner turns out, and Smiley told us that when he's criticized by a customer it really hurts, so he tries to get everything perfect.

We should add that "Smiley" is no misnomer. Everyone at the Agawam was quite friendly, and we got several examples of diner humor. For example, when we asked if they had been working hard in the kitchen, the reply was, "You've heard of the Golden Arches? Well, we've got the fallen arches."

There's a complete bakery in the diner's basement. When we went down there to look around, Jimmy had just finished for the day. A wonderful array of pastries covered the table: raspberry Danish, mocha cake, apple and raspberry turnovers, brownies, cupcakes, chocolate log rolls with buttercream filling, apple squares with vanilla icing, raspberry leaf tarts, banana and coconut cream pies, lemon meringue pies, blueberry pie, custard pie, and, in season, strawberry-rhubarb pie.

The Agawam also makes its own soups and chowders from scratch. Seafood available includes fried shrimp, clams, and scallops. There is a combination fish plate served with fresh coleslaw and french fries that goes for about $3.00. Greek lamb, baked in tomato sauce and served with rice pilaf, is one of the specials. Other specials include individual chicken pies made with peas and carrots but no potatoes, and beef stew. The meat and the vegetables for the stew are cooked separately and then combined in the broth, which is thickened with a little tomato paste. Smiley told us that the stew sold for 25 cents when the diner first opened; now we're happy if it's under $2.00.

This shiny stainless steel diner does most of its business in the summer months. Like many businesses that get the bulk of their trade from tourists, prices are slightly lower during the off-season. But whatever the time of year, a trip to the Agawam is a pleasant and satisfying experience.

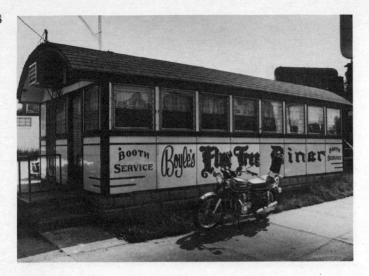

## Boyle's Elm Tree Diner

*Salem, Massachusetts*

When we arrived at Boyle's Elm Tree it was closing time. The whole family was there. Don was working behind the counter while his wife, Peggy, was sitting on a stool and playing with their infant grandaughter on the marble counter top. Three of their five kids work at the diner, but the other two were also there when we made our visits. The ones who were working were washing down everything. And we mean everything: the blades of the exhaust fan behind the ancient grill, the white porcelain walls, the steam tables—all spotless.

If Hansel and Gretel ate at a diner, it would have to be this one. The Elm Tree is a Worcester Lunch Car, built in the 1920s. There's no kitchen out back; all the cooking is done up front, where you can watch. If you're eating at a booth, or the counter, you dine at a marble tabletop. The booths themselves are high-backed and made from oak. This is the only diner we found that still had original tabletops. Don's been offered lots of money for the marble but always refused. The son of a diner owner, and now a diner owner himself, he's maintained a love for the old-time diner and the old-time diner way of doing things.

This place is small, almost like a bungalow, but it is gorgeous. Something that we never saw before was the enormous hand-carved mahogany menu case hanging above the grill. There are curved transom windows above the doors at each end of the diner. The base of the counter is white porcelain, the wall behind the grill—and the fridge alongside—are the same porcelain, and the floor is a black-and-white checked tile. Coffee is served in thick eight-ounce mugs, instead of the usual seven-ounce, and is constantly being warmed up when the mugs become half empty.

The menu at Boyle's is limited, as are the hours, and breakfast is the big meal. Omlettes such as Western or ham and cheese are popular, and the thick slices of French toast are a house specialty. Because everything is stored and prepared behind the counter, there is little variety. Hamburgers and hamburg steak are available, along with the sandwich menu.

Don told us that he doesn't understand why people will eat in a pancake house and pay a dollar or two more for the same breakfast they can get at his diner. We don't understand it either.

Don and Peggy close their diner every summer for a two-week vacation, usually at the end of July or the beginning of August. Since the diner is too small to even have a wall phone, there's no way to call in advance and make sure they're open, but if you're in the area it's definitely worth taking a chance and stopping by. You don't get the chance to see a diner like this every day.

*Don and Peggy with one of their sons*

## Salem Diner

*Salem, Massachusetts*

The Salem Diner, which was built by the Sterling Company in 1941, looks like something that just landed. It's so stream-lined it seems extraterrestrial. One end of the building curves out at a slant, like the front of a diesel locomotive. This was a conscious design on the part of the Sterling people. Advertisements for their diners would superimpose their latest models alongside an airplane and a train. There's a Sterling diner in Providence, Rhode Island, called the Yankee Clipper, named after the famous 1939 flying machine. The creator of this curvilinear diner combined a sense of art-deco elegance with the feeling of power that the new planes and trains promised for the modern age.

When we entered the Salem Diner we were greeted by one of the workers, Napolean Leblanc, or Nap, as he's called, who was stationed behind the glass-topped counter. Nap was back in the diner business after a long absence; he had been working at the Salem on its opening day. He told us that the diner was so busy in its heyday that the door would have to be locked to keep the people out. Opening day for the Salem was July 3, 1941. The way Nap tells the story, that weekend was the biggest thing in town since the witch burnings.

"I worked here three days, three nights, without going home, with two other men washing dishes—the three of us. That's how busy it was. It never let up, day or night, because we were open twenty-four hours a day then. It never let up for three days or three nights because it was a holiday, like a weekend, you know. You opened up around three o'clock in the afternoon the day before the Fourth. And it was a holiday the next day, and that place kept jammin' and jumpin' all the way through, day and night. We'd take turns at taking snoozes down in the cellar."

Nap blames the increased use of the automobile for the decline in the diner's popularity. Back when cars were scarce, couples would have to double and triple up on dates, and after the movies they'd all go someplace together for a late snack, usually the diner. Now that everyone has a car, people just don't go out in groups as much. It's an interesting theory, even if we're not sure we agree.

The interior of the Salem Diner is as beautiful as the outside, and it's very well maintained. In addition to the glass-topped counter, the diner features a white barreled roof, and the walls beneath the windows are an ivory-colored metal. The checkered floor is in shades of green mosaic, and there is a large green horseshoe-shaped booth at the curved end of the diner. The menus carry a logo of a witch on her broomstick, and you should look as you enter for the well-worn Sterling diner emblem that is set into the doorstep.

The Salem offers a very full and reasonably priced menu. Fried seafood is popular; we tried the fried smelts and thought they were fresh and very good. Other fried fish include shrimp, scallops, clam, and haddock. We also had such diner standards as the American chop suey and New England boiled dinner, and we weren't disappointed with either dish. The Salem offers a large breakfast menu. It also has the usual full assortment of burgers and sandwiches, as well as lobster, crabmeat, and chicken salad sandwiches. All the pastries are baked at the diner. Squash pie, mince pie, cherry tarts, and other delicious desserts are available, as well as homemade muffins.

The Salem is one of our favorite diners. It's the first place we ever had American chop suey, years ago. Never having heard of the dish before, we decided to try it. When the counterman brought out the platter, we were surprised. "We ordered chop suey," we told him, "not spaghetti." He was peeved. "What are you, Russian or somethin'?" he snapped back. When we told Nap this story he was amused. It seems he ran into a similar problem in another diner, where that dish was called "escalloped hamburger." We were glad we weren't the only ones who had fallen victim to the varieties of diner lingo.

*The current Boulevard*

## Boulevard Diner

*Worcester, Massachusetts*

For many years Worcester was the center of diner manufacturing in New England, and Worcesterites take their diner heritage seriously. When they speak of old dinermen like Joe Kirby or Fred J. Galanto, it's with great reverence and respect. These men invented and developed many of the concepts of diner operation that are still used today.

John George, owner of the Boulevard Diner, studied under legendary dinerman Fred J. Galanto, who originally owned the Boulevard. When John speaks of Mr. Galanto, it's with an enthusiasm and deference that he reserves for special individuals.

John puts a lot of care into the preparation of the food that he serves. The Boulevard is well known for its Italian meals, and everything there is made from scratch. Even the sausages are made by John in the diner's kitchen, on the same sausage machine that has been in the diner since it first opened in 1936.

The Boulevard was custom-built to Fred Galanto's specifications and features many fine details, such as the wooden hat racks over each wooden booth. These racks are exact replicas of those found in old railroad cars. The windows in the diner are all made from beveled glass, which acts as a mirror. This was done by the original owner so that he would be able to observe from the kitchen what was happening along the entire length of the building, reflected in the windows. John says that Mr. Galanto "was a guy who was on top of everything."

We saw a photo of the old diner that used to be on the same spot where the Boulevard is now. Taken in 1926, it shows Mr. Galanto standing proudly in a lunch wagon that also served as a general store. One thing that hasn't changed over the years is the Kellogg's cereal display that is visible in the old photo and can still be seen in the "new" diner.

John told us about the day they brought the Boulevard in on wheels. "I was ten years old," he told us. "Then when I worked here I dreamed I was going to own the diner some day, and my dream came true. I really dreamed to myself that the day was going to come when I would be the sole owner."

He spoke about the years he worked in the kitchen. He says he started as a dishwasher and "worked in the kitchen for seven years. I kept my mouth shut and listened. I love to listen for smart and good advice."

Besides putting in seven years in the kitchen, John has been working behind the counter for an additional twenty-six years, so he knows the diner business inside out. He has his two daughters and a son helping him now.

When John took us into the kitchen, we were thrilled by the sight and smell of all that good food cooking. There were three huge cast-iron skillets sitting on the stove. One of them contained the onions, peppers, tomatoes, and garlic that go into his meat loaf. John buys only choice ground beef for his meat loaf, showing us a receipt he had gotten that day from the butcher, marked "extra lean," to prove it.

The other two skillets held homemade sausage. John uses grease from the sausage to cook his home fries, which are

*The original Boulevard Diner, 1926. (Courtesy of John George)*

74  delicious. There was a huge pot of homemade spaghetti sauce also simmering on the stove. He also makes his own meatballs, which he mashes up to use as filling for his lasagna. When we ate the sausage and pasta, which is very reasonably priced, we were served a bowlful of grated cheese to go with it.

We asked John if he felt any competition from the fast-food chains, and his reply was that with "my food, nobody's gonna touch me. It's all good Italian cooking."

There's a full breakfast menu, including French toast, oatmeal, and pancakes. Home fries are extra with your eggs, but breakfast is still a decent buy at about $1.00.

John feels that he's part of the community, and he likes to involve himself in civic projects. The diner sponsors the basketball team for Assumption College.

The Boulevard is a Worcester landmark, one that's famous throughout the town, and we look forward to going back many more times.

*Inside the present-day Boulevard*

*Fred J. Galanto inside the original Boulevard, circa 1926.*
*(Courtesy of John George)*

## Miss Worcester

*Worcester, Massachusetts*

Larry Ciccolo, one of the owners of the Miss Worcester, was hesitant about being interviewed. He felt that he had been misquoted before by others, and we had to work hard to convince him of our diner integrity before he'd agree to meet with us. The entire time we were there, his basic suspiciousness never left him. The first part of the interview was conducted across a table in the kitchen. Larry, who's dark-haired, somewhere between thirty and forty years old, and built like a brick wall, stood over a slab of beef, dressed in his whites and wielding a very large and very sharp knife. With rapid movements he trimmed the fat from his stew meat while he interrogated us about our intentions. When we finally got through to him, he adopted a manner that we assumed—for him anyway—could be termed "friendly."

There's a rumor around that the Miss Worcester is the first Worcester Lunch Car ever built—not true, but it does have an interesting history. Situated across the street from the site of the old lunch car factory, it served for years as a working demonstration to prospective buyers of what the standard Worcester Lunch Car was like. This diner, with its barreled roof, marble counter, enameled exterior, and up-front grill, is a classic example of what the Worcester people were building in the 1930s and 1940s. And Larry, who's proud of his skill as a grillman, is a classic dinerman.

"My partner and myself are the two best grillmen that

you'll see in Worcester," Larry told us. "I say Worcester because I haven't been outside," he added. We asked him what the secret of being a good grillman is, and he told us that the main thing is the rhythm. It's not quick movements but rather no wasted motion. He said that the most important thing is to keep the grill clean—no greasy eggs—and that the ideal grill area is "clean, neat, well stocked, so that you can go and go and go." We also asked Larry why there were more men working grills than women. His reply was that the grillman is a stereotype that woman are breaking, and he has a woman, Donna, working the grill in the morning.

The Miss Worcester, which is open twenty-four hours five days a week, serves a large cross section of the Worcester population. We met at least one bona fide millionaire seated among the factory workers at the counter. Lots of students from Holy Cross eat there, and cab drivers, bartenders, and waitresses make up a big part of the crowd at night. Boston Celtic Kevin Stacom eats there, and the rock group Led Zeppelin behaved themselves while indulging in some of the diner's excellent stew.

Different specials are available daily. Tuesday is American chop suey day, and Thursday is traditional for corned beef and cabbage. Larry and his partner, George, also make their own chicken pies, which are prepared as individual servings. And they make their own gravy and mashed potatoes. All the meats are fresh, but the soups are canned. Ingredients are added to beef up the soups, though—Larry says they're 60 percent him and 40 percent Campbell's. Other daily specials include roast pork (which roasts in its own juices), meat loaf, roast chicken, and braised beef. All these dinners include potato, vegetable, and bread and butter and are priced at under $3.00. The beef stew, which is a big seller, contains potatoes, carrots, and celery. Last time we looked, the stew went for $1.50.

The corner of Quinsigamond Avenue and Southbridge Street, where the Miss Worcester stands, is purely industrial. The ancient gray and red-brick factories surrounding the diner are up for landmark-building status, so typical are they of industrial Worcester. Along Southbridge Street there's a railroad trestle that runs above the diner. The entire vista seems appropriate for a diner setting, and Larry seems to be the perfect dinerman for this diner. We couldn't say that the Miss Worcester is our favorite, but its history and location give it a special quality.

# New Hampshire

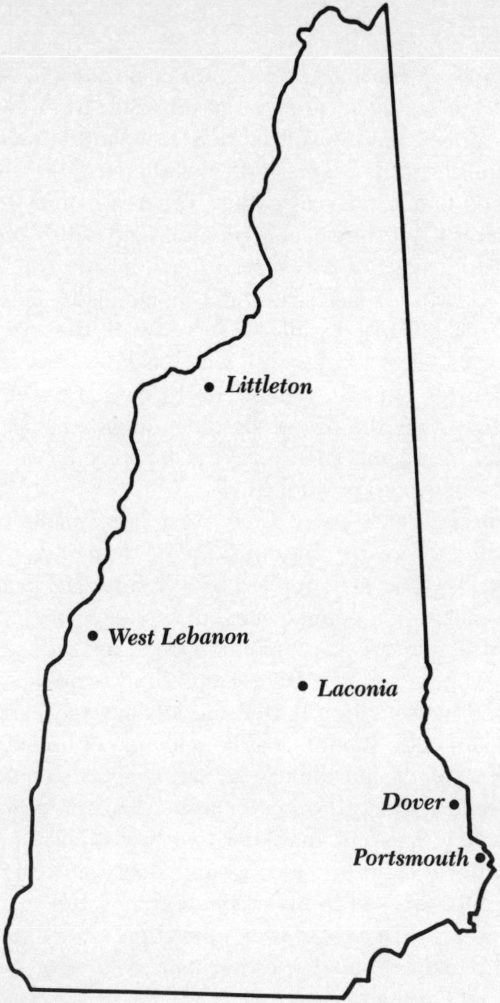

- Littleton
- West Lebanon
- Laconia
- Dover
- Portsmouth

*Dover, New Hampshire*

We first heard of Stoney's many years ago from our good friend Eric Rosenthal, who insisted that we come up for some of Stoney's chicken croquettes. Once we'd tried them, we always planned a stop at this diner whenever visiting south-eastern New Hampshire. Stoney passed away last year, and Marsha Stone now runs her late husband's diner. She's kept everything the same in this 1958 Masters diner, including the recipe for the famous croquettes.

From the outside, Stoney's looks like your classic, plain, stainless steel diner, with plenty of windows. Inside, it's a festival of pink and pearl. The recessed ceiling is pink Formica, and it curves at the corners. The floor is tiled pink, and the counter top and tabletops are pearl-colored Formica. The tables have a pink trim along the surface, and the counter top shows the gradual erosion caused by thousands of elbows over the years.

The diner sits just a few feet away from the Boston and Maine Railroad tracks. If you're there at the right time of day, you can watch a long freight train roll by on its way to Canada. And if you're unself-conscious enough to wave to the engineer, you'll be pleased to see he'll wave right back. Naturally, Stoney's gets its share of railroad workers; sometimes the train will stop and they'll run in for coffee. And a fair number of truckers and travelers stop by, as the word goes out over the CB radios that this is *the* place to eat in coastal New Hampshire.

Stoney, who started in the diner business with a fourteen-stool lunch wagon, always served good, fresh food at reasonable prices, and this tradition still continues. Besides the croquettes, other specialties include potted beef, sirloin tips, braised beef, and veal cutlet. The veal comes to the restaurant fresh, not frozen, and is tenderized with a meat pounder.

Fish dishes are also served here, mostly fried. Fish cakes, served with french fries and homemade coleslaw, go for about $2.00. Fried scallops, served with the same vegetables, go for $4.00. A lobster roll, which is lobster salad served on a frankfurter bun, is available on Fridays. One of the favorites at Stoney's is the oyster stew, made with whole oysters and plenty of cream. There are also beef croquettes, ham steak, fried clams, and pickled tripe.

For dessert, choose from such homemade treats as rice pudding, bread pudding, and homemade strawberry shortcake. Pies are supplied by a commercial baker.

Breakfast is a popular meal at Stoney's Diner, and there is an attractive breakfast menu. Decorated with a picture of a sun with a smiling face, colored illustrations of pancakes topped with melting butter and lots of syrup, and a platter of ham and eggs, it offers a large selection of breakfast foods.

Most of the customers at Stoney's are regulars. We saw one fellow, Booty Forbes, who used to come in four times a day. Now he's cut that down to twice daily, ever since his daughter bought him a coffeepot. Booty's usually there in the morning, dressed in his working greens and suspenders. But whether you're a regular or a first-time visitor to this stainless steel paradise, Marsha, or her twin sister, Pat, will make you feel right at home.

## Paugus Diner

*Laconia, New Hampshire*

A Worcester Lunch Car that was built about forty years ago, the Paugus Diner is famous both for its fish and for its dessert pies. Originally located in Concord, New Hampshire, the diner was hauled into Laconia on its own wheels some twenty years ago. As in other towns, the bringing of the diner to its new location was a big event that brought the whole town out.

The sign on the sandwich board outside reads: WELCOME TO CARL AND NORMA'S PAUGUS DINER. HOPE YOU ENJOY YOUR MEAL. Carl and Norma Blacky are a husband-and-wife team who've been in the restaurant business for quite some time, although they've owned the Paugus for only a few years. The diner is a family operation, with their daughters and other assorted relatives all working together. However, Norma, who loves to cook, does almost all the cooking. The reports are that even at home she spends most of her time at the stove.

Perhaps the most striking feature of the diner's interior is its marble counter, which is a much darker shade of brown than you'll find in most Worcester Lunch Cars. It's kept sparkling clean and highly polished. There is also a sign inside that tells you that you are in a "respectable establishment" and that you must be "properly attired."

True to the tradition of fine diners everywhere, all the foods at Paugus Diner are cooked fresh on the premises. Fresh fish is a big item. Clams, scallops, and haddock are all available, fried or baked. Fish and clam chowders are served, usually on Fridays, and occasionally there is oyster stew. One fish dish we particularly enjoyed was the salmon pie. Prepared in a rather plain style, it was nevertheless tasty and very filling. Made from canned salmon, the meat is cooked inside a pie crust and topped with cream sauce; the crust is very light, and the sauce is mild in flavor.

This is a potluck diner. With few exceptions (boiled dinner on Thursday, American chop suey on Monday) there is no set schedule for daily specials. Norma just cooks them as she feels like it. One of the big items is the chicken fingers. These are made of boneless breast of chicken cut into strips, breaded, and deep-fried. There is also something called "Chinaman's Pie"; hamburger and corn are cooked together and covered with pie crust in individual pie servings. The spaghetti sauce is homemade, and the roast stuffed turkey is so popular that five large birds are cooked every week. The stuffing could be bread stuffing or meat or even cranberry, depending on how the cook feels. Other roasts offered are pork roast, pot roast, and roast beef. Meat loaf is the perennial diner favorite. Carl makes pork chow mein, which we didn't try; it's served with rice or noodles.

There are at least two salad plates available regularly: macaroni salad, in which the pasta is mixed with tuna fish, and a potato salad plate, which comes with a side order of ham or franks as well as tomato and cucumber.

The freshly made soups include vegetable beef, minestrone, and fish and clam chowders. We tried the fish chowder and were a little disappointed. There wasn't as much milk in the soup base as we would have liked, and it was too thin in comparison to most of the chowders we had in other New England diners.

All the desserts are baked right there, and, like the daily specials, the selection is always unpredictable. You might find a chocolate cream, or date cream, or peanut-butter cream pie, or apple, blueberry, raspberry, or apricot pie. The rice pudding is made with pineapple in it. All pie fillings come out of a can.

Breakfast muffins are baked on the premises, too, and include banana date, cherry bran, and strawberry muffins.

We spoke to the dishwasher, Della, who has been washing the diner's dishes for over twenty-years, and asked her about the temptation of all the good food that's always around her in the kitchen, but she told us, "I don't eat nothin'." Everyone agreed that Della eats like a bird, of which she happens to own two—parakeets. She also had, at last count, fifty-two goldfish and a little white dog named Judy. A pet store was being built behind the diner when we were there, so maybe Della has added to her stock by now.

## Littleton Diner

*Littleton, New Hampshire*

Located above Franconia Notch in the heart of New Hampshire's White Mountains, Littleton is a resort town year-round. Vacationers appreciate its scenic beauty, and skiers thrive on the deep New England snows. The Littleton Diner has been serving all these people for thirty-five years.

The diner was on the downslide before Dennis Fekay, its present owner, took over. The previous owners seem to have been religious fanatics, and the place had gotten a reputation as a "Bible belt" diner. Customers would be bombarded with quotes from the Scriptures and sermons from behind the counter. This type of thing tends to limit the clientele. Also, the appearance of the place had become run-down.

Dennis, who is a large man with black hair and beard, broadened the outlook of the diner by adding a restaurant in the back and introducing some unusual dishes. He also made some necessary renovations in the diner area, cleaning it up.

The Littleton Diner is a Sterling diner built in the 1940s. Even though there have been quite a few changes both inside and out, many of the original Sterling trademarks remain. The grill is gone, but the glass counter, a rarity these days, is still there; its base is an ivory enamel decorated with a red geometric pattern. The stools are all original, with their octagonal bases; the wooden booths are there, and the barreled ceiling is of white enamel ribbed with mahogany strips. The milk-glass ceiling globes give off the warm glow of a 1940s diner.

Dennis moved to Littleton from the Philadelphia area about fifteen years ago. He tried a little of everything to make a living, working as a florist and a lumberjack and at other odd jobs, but nothing quite grabbed him like the diner business. He enjoys meeting new people, joking with the regulars, and the "fast life" of the grill. There's no other way to go, according to Dennis.

There are two menus, one for the diner itself, and another larger (and more expensive) menu for the dining room. Dennis is of Middle Eastern descent, and he has several foods from that part of the world on the menu. Baked kibbe is one such dish, made from choice ground beef and crushed wheat, gently spiced and baked. Steak kabob is another, made from marinated slices of steak cut thick, cooked on a skewer, and served on a bed of rice. Both dishes come with an Arabic salad (called *taboul*), potato, and hot pita bread and were priced at $6.00 and $8.00 respectively. These dishes are listed on the dining room menu but are also available in the diner.

Seafood is plentiful at the Littleton Diner. We tried broiled scallops and were pleased to find that they were not only tasty and succulent but also served in a very attractive fashion. The scallops come in a separate casserole dish, which is placed on a plate with a vegetable (we had the coleslaw; more on that later) and parsley sprigs.

There are plenty of sandwiches on the menu, including a favorite of ours, the hoagie. A hoagie, which originated in Philadelphia, is quite similar to what is referred to in other parts of the country as a submarine sandwich or a hero, but it is definitely a cut above the rest. There are at least five different types of burgers on the menu, as well as barbecued beef and pork. All sandwiches are served with potato chips and pickles.

The coleslaw is unusual and has an excellent flavor. It's sweeter than most, and the carrots and cabbage that go into it are sliced into thick strips. The french fries are the real thing, not frozen, and we highly recommend the salad dressing, which is a sweet Italian made with a touch of maple syrup.

Speaking of maple syrup, for breakfast you can have blueberry, peach, or pear pancakes, or French toast. Also available are fresh donuts, cinnamon toast, and homemade muffins.

The White Mountains of New Hampshire are truly a beautiful sight. If you've never seen them, it's worth the trip, and if you have, then you know just what we mean. When you do go, take this book along so you won't forget to stop off at Dennis's diner. Tell him Don and Al sent you.

*Gilly's Lunch Wagon*

## Gilly's Lunch Wagon

*Portsmouth, New Hampshire*

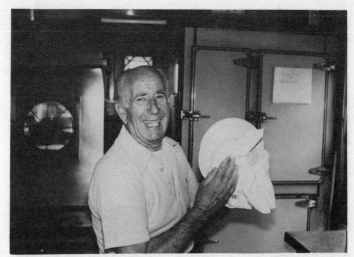

*Gilly Gilbert*

Like Portsmouth itself, Gilly's is a diner that's rich in history. Named after Gilly Gilbert, who still works there part-time, this is the only lunch cart we ever heard of that was reputed to have been in the *Guinness Book of World Records*. Every day Gilly's used to be hauled out into the center of town on the back of a truck at 5:00 P.M., where Gilly would dish out franks and beans until five in the morning and then depart. Parked illegally, it would be ticketed regularly, but no one ever bothered to make Gilly pay up. It is for the greatest consecutive number of parking tickets—over five thousand—that the lunch wagon was supposedly listed in *Guinness*.

Now in his seventies, with a ruddy glow to his complexion and bushy white eyebrows, Gilly has to be the fastest "dog man" in the East. He never stops moving behind the counter; even when no one's ordering, he's busy cleaning, preparing, or arranging something.

This wagon, according to Gilly (who's a local historian, in addition to everything else), is the last hauled lunch cart that came out of the Worcester Lunch Car factory. You enter through a sliding door or order takeout through a side window. Inside, it's all oak and yellow enamel. Even the pie racks are wooden. There is a portable copper drain beneath the coffee urn. Gilly's eyes gleamed when he recalled the

*A customer at Gilly's*

original nickel-plated urn. "It was a handsome piece," he said.

When Gilly serves out a platter of franks and beans on one of his green or blue plates, he'll squirt a little mustard on top. He's served over seven million dogs in the more than thirty years the lunch cart's been in existence. There's a small tray full of condiments on the counter: mustard, ketchup, hot sauce, salt, pepper, celery sauce, and sugar. Napkins are neatly stacked in a pinwheel-like swirl on top of the counter, which makes it easy to pick them up. It's the little touches.

A few years ago, when Gilly went into semi-retirement, the town proclaimed Gilly Gilbert Day in his honor. There was a parade led by the mayor, front-page headlines, and the gift of a brand-new automobile.

Gilly knows everyone in town, and several of his younger customers told us how their dads used to eat there or, in one case, work there. People come in to warm up with a dog and a cup of coffee, sit in the back of this eleven-stooler, and admire Gilly's fleet-fingered dexterity as he moves around the small grill and steam box. An order to go is quickly wrapped in wax paper and tied with string.

Gilly can describe in amazing detail the glory days of Portsmouth, when it was a great shipbuilding town. He recalls fondly the times when the town was full of blue-and-white uniforms and still remembers the time the submarine sank in the harbor back in 1936—or was it 1937?

There was a time when shipbuilding, especially submarine-building, was the big topic of conversation. Gilly says, "They built submarines in here. Never got 'em out the door, but built as many as in the shipyards." Today there's a TV set in one corner, and the big topic of conversation is likely to be whether or not the Bruins are going to make it to the Stanley Cup or why the Red Sox rehired Don Zimmer.

The lunch wagon still sits on the back of a beat-up old truck, which has 2,200 miles on it—a quarter mile per day—but it is now parked permanently behind the main shopping center. You can feel the rumble of the compressor underneath as you order your dog or burger or have a piece of pie with your coffee. There was a time when everything served here was a local product, but today the small businesses are gone. You can tell this saddens Gilly, but he rolls with the punches.

If you wish to see Gilly himself in action, stop by the wagon on a Sunday, Monday, or Tuesday, after 7:30 P.M. It's a one-man show.

## Four Aces Diner

*West Lebanon, New Hampshire*

We had heard about the neon sign outside the Four Aces Diner from several different sources, all of whom raved about it, so it was with some sense of anticipation that we looked forward to seeing this fabled neon extravaganza. The sign depicted four aces and flashed at night in different colors. Unfortunately, the sign had other admirers who wanted it for their private collection. Before we arrived it had been spirited away by some Dartmouth boys as part of a fraternity prank and never recovered. We were disappointed to find it missing, but grillman Sheldon Gomez seemed philosophical about the whole thing. He seemed more impressed that they had gotten away with it than outraged. It was very large and very heavy.

The Four Aces is a late-model Worcester Lunch Car, one of only half a dozen or so we know of with a stainless steel exterior. The interior is a wonderful mixture of wood, enamel, and stainless steel. The barreled ceiling is pink enamel, the booths and window frames are wood, the wall behind the counter is yellow enamel, and the grill hood and sandwich board are made from stainless steel. The frame around the sandwich board is decorated with a sunburst pattern.

The tabletops are a light-tan Formica, reminiscent of the shade of marble that was used in older Worcester diners. They are trimmed with red, another favorite color of the

Worcester people. The outside walls of the diner are decorated with vertical stripes of red enamel. These broad red stripes are also visible in the dining room, which the owners themselves added on to one side of the building; what was an outside wall became an inside wall once the addition was constructed.

Several of the small touches in construction that we always appreciate are the official rectangular Worcester clock that is mounted on a wooden arch at one end of the ceiling, the wooden cupboard and candy case, which are situated by the entrance and which also hold the cash register, and the interior of the entranceway, built with stainless steel and wood.

The clientele at the Four Aces is a mixed bag of locals and college students. This is Dartmouth territory, and quite a few students appreciate good diner food. Many townspeople eat two meals a day at the Four Aces. Gravy seems to be a favorite with some of these folks, and it's not uncommon to hear someone ask for an extra "ten cents' worth of gravy."

We knew we had a good diner to visit when we spoke to William Syms, who runs a junk shop right next door to the Four Aces. The sunburned Mr. Syms, before becoming the purveyor of discarded objects, had the mail-truck run from St. Johnsbury, Vermont, to the southern part of that state. During that period of time he joined the circle of Vermont diner cognoscente. He told us that he had never found a better diner than the Four Aces. Today he takes full advantage of the proximity of his shop to the diner and eats lunch there every day.

It's real New England home cooking at the Four Aces: fresh coleslaw, chicken dishes made from whole chickens—the works. The diner is famous for its pork chops, which, served with potato, vegetable, and coleslaw, go for about $3.00. Once a week there's a stuffed pork chop special. Served with vegetable, potato, applesauce, and dessert, the pork chop special costs about $2.00.

If you visit the Four Aces, be sure and stop by Mr. Syms's junk shop next door. Who knows? Maybe you'll be lucky enough to find some diner memorabilia.

# New Jersey

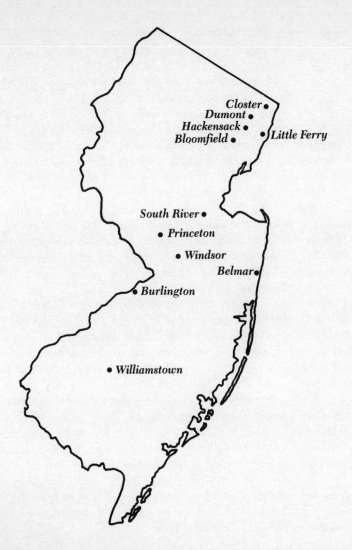

Closter •
Dumont •
Hackensack •
Bloomfield • • Little Ferry

South River •
• Princeton
• Windsor
Belmar •
• Burlington
• Williamstown

*Belmar, New Jersey*

Pat's Riverview is a diner that wishes it weren't. When the parents of the present owners ran it as a true diner, it was called Pat's Deluxe Diner, and a deluxe diner it must have been. Today, the stainless steel Fodero exterior, which still gleams with all its beauty, is almost all that's left of the original. The counter has been redone, along with the booths, and a dining room and bar have been added. But the ceiling is the same Formica that came with the building almost thirty years ago, and the area where the telephones and immaculate rest rooms are is vintage diner tile.

In spite of all that's been done to disguise this diner, including strict portion control, its origins are unmistakable and its location is quite beautiful. The windows along the booths offer an excellent view of the harbor, complete with piers and fishing boats. The salty sea air tells you that good seafood should be available, and it is. Fish is the house specialty at Pat's Riverview.

The food at this diner is basically good, if parsimoniously portioned. Pat's has three different menus: lunch, breakfast, and dinner. Each is quite extensive and nicely illustrated. The food could not be called cheap, but there is plenty to choose from.

At breakfast time, fresh fruits and hot and cold cereals are available. There are pancakes and French toast, three-egg omelettes served with home fries and toast (omelettes such as Swiss cheese, Western, and mushroom). There is also a large selection of breakfast meats that includes bacon, pork roll, sausage links, Virginia ham, Canadian bacon, and rib steak. Continental breakfast is served for slightly over $1.00. There is a 75-cent minimum for table service.

Most of the items offered at breakfast are available at lunchtime, with the addition of a full selection of burgers and sandwiches. Homemade soups are also served at lunch, as are such hot platters as fried fillet of sole, roast turkey, and pork chops. At lunchtime the minimum per person at the booths is 85 cents.

The dinner menu is the longest, offering almost everything that's available in the morning and the afternoon and then adding about thirty different entrées, eleven appetizers (including chopped liver, spaghetti with meat sauce, and shrimp cocktail), eleven different vegetables, and a full array of fresh-baked desserts.

At dinner time we recommend that you stick to the seafood. The roast leg of veal was all right, but the homemade mushroom gravy tasted thick and canned. It was served with coleslaw that was good and mashed potatoes that were also okay. The turkey pie was seved as an individual pie in a ceramic dish. The turkey meat was plentiful and the potatoes and vegetables helped to make a good filling, but the cream sauce was basically tasteless.

As we said, fish is what the Riverview does best, and we found the scallops to be quite good. We also recommend the pan-fried smelts, the oysters, and the broiled fillet of sole. You can have all these together on a seafood combination platter. But whatever you do, stay away from the bean salad that's placed on every table; it tastes like the beans were pickled in formaldehyde.

All baking is done on the premises, including the breakfast muffins. We had cherry pie and blueberry pie and found the filling to be incredibly sweet, while the crust was light, tender, and delicious. We also found the bread pudding to be most acceptable.

On your way out to the parking lot, catch the neon sign that says FOOD THAT'S FINER. It's a remnant from the original diner decor, and it will make you yearn for the days when a well-worn grill was a dinerman's most prized possession and he proudly presented it up front in full view of the customers, instead of banishing it to the back of the kitchen in shameful obscurity.

## Short Stop Diner

*Bloomfield, New Jersey*

The Short Stop is the home of "eggs in a skillet." It's also a prime example of the diner as the original fast-food restaurant. A small establishment built in 1953 by the Manno Dining Car Company, it has only eighteen stools yet can serve up to three hundred customers in an eight-hour shift.

It was built originally as part of a chain of diners; there's another Short Stop in Belleville, New Jersey. Manufactured by a local firm no longer in business, the Short Stop is all glass and stainless steel on the outside, with stripes of colored enamel that further brighten its already brilliant facade. Inside, the diner is too small for booths. In addition to the usual diner counter, there are two smaller counters that run along the plate-glass windows. The limited menu consists almost entirely of eggs and burgers.

The manager of the Short Stop, Pete Fisher, struck us as a very nervous guy. Maybe it's all the coffee he drinks, or perhaps it's the pressure of running a business that's open twenty-four hours a day, seven days a week, closing only on Christmas Day. Thin, dark-haired, and goateed, Pete told us he had worked in a bank for fourteen years before joining his uncle in the diner business in 1973. He pointed toward the parking lot as he explained the Short Stop philosophy.

"We have a sign out there that says 'fifteen-minute parking for customers only.' And we believe in 'eat it and beat it.' We serve them nice. They get good food, good service, but we want them out of here, because you're so small you can't have people sit here for an hour, an hour and a half. It's not that kind of establishment."

When Pete talks about the Short Stop, he refers to the corporation. He takes a strong professional view toward the running of his business, and he uses a great deal of quality control. For example, he sends his ground meat out once or twice a month to a lab, to check on the fat content and to make sure it's as lean as his suppliers claim. The coffee he serves is a special blend that costs more than he might have to pay for other coffees, but he believes in high quality. And you can taste the difference. While we were there, some cops came in to eat. We were told that they were from two towns away and that they drive past four other diners just to come to the Short Stop for coffee.

The trademark of the Short Stop (besides "eat it and beat it") is "eggs in a skillet." All eggs and omelettes are cooked in butter in their own individual skillets. Then they are served in the skillet, which rests on a wooden plate. The eggs are undercooked just a drop, because they'll keep on cooking in the pan while they sit in front of you. One reason for serving them this way is that the diner's grill is very small, and this way the eggs don't pick up the flavor of anything else that might be cooking.

There's no such thing as a breakfast special at this twenty-four-hour diner. The prices ran this way when we were there (of course, in this age of inflation they could be going up while you're reading this): two eggs, 70 cents; coffee, 35 cents per cup; bacon or ham, 80 cents; potatoes, 50 cents. So the full breakfast meal, including meat, would run you about $2.50. Two types of ham are available, Taylor and smoked, and steak and eggs are served. The steak is ground beef, and this platter comes with coffee for just under $4.00.

Most of the help at the Short Stop has been employed there for years, and they're all fast workers. "Everything we have we cook in a matter of seconds," says Pete "Not minutes, seconds." Besides the eggs, it's mainly burgers; there is no kitchen to turn out dinners. The soup is canned. Pete made a big deal about his hash brown potatoes, refusing to reveal his secret recipe. When we tried them, however, (they're served pancake-style) we found them to be quite ordinary.

On weekends, the Short Stop is a favorite for families out shopping. There's also a large college crowd, and many workers from local industries eat there on all shifts. We recommend it for a quick bite, and the coffee is hard to beat.

## Burlington Diner

*Burlington, New Jersey*

*Inside the Burlington Diner: note the ceiling fans and mosaic floor*

Not only is the Burlington Diner unusually long—because it's actually two diners end to end—but it has a full-size dining room as well. The dining room is mostly used by the bus loads of shoppers who come from as far away as Maryland. Burlington, New Jersey, has many discount outlet stores, and groups will charter buses for the sole purpose of taking advantage of the bargains the outlets offer. The shoppers invariably stop at this diner for some good buys on fine food too.

The Burlington was the first diner on Route 130, according to Gus Mastoris and John Stratis, the owners. Originally built by the De Raffele Company, it started out as a single diner but soon built a reputation as an excellent eating place. A second diner was joined to the first to accommodate the many customers. Only one of the diner halves has a counter, however; the other contains booths. A seam in the mosaic floor where the two were joined is clearly visible. The floors are tiled with a dizzying pattern that resembles an M.C. Escher print, and the barreled ceilings are made from a shining enamel that, like the rest of the diner, is kept spotless. A row of ceiling fans hangs along the center of the diner.

*The candy counter*

The menu at the Burlington is as extensive as the diner is long. Everything is made from scratch with fresh ingredients, and the food is of superior quality. We noticed something called Irish beef stew and wondered just what made it different from ordinary beef stew. We were pleasantly surprised, when we tried it, to discover that it's cooked in a white cream base and richly flavored with dill. We also enjoyed the chicken pot pie, which has a light and delicate top crust and came with a side order of the Burlington's own coleslaw. Both the stew and the pot pie were reasonably priced at about $3.50.

Other specials included Polish kielbasa with potato and sauerkraut, chicken or Virginia ham croquettes, cheese ravioli, baked sausage, barbecued chicken, corned beef on rye, and lasagna. The average price for all these dishes is slightly over $3.00, and they all come with vegetables of your choice from their large selection.

The seafood specials are also numerous. Everything is cooked with great care. For instance, the mackerel is broiled in a light lemon sauce, as is the baby flounder. Fillet of flounder and flounder with seafood stuffing are other seafood offerings. Even stuffed lobster tails are available, as well as a fried oyster plate, fried deviled crab, and broiled, fried, or stuffed fried shrimp. Fish prices run somewhat higher than the other entrées.

You'll find a full sandwich selection, several types of club sandwiches, and a children's menu. The kids can have a Davy Crockett (chopped steak platter), a Peter Pan (frankfurter platter), or a Tinkerbell (turkey platter). The Burlington serves a large variety of milk shakes, including a malted with egg, ice-cream sodas, and sundaes.

All baked goods are made on the premises, not only the

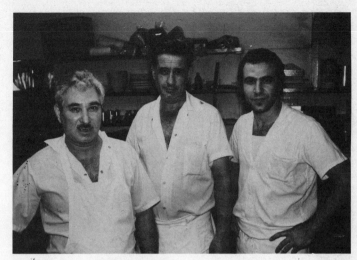

*The crew at the Burlington Diner*

94  pies but also the delicious cheesecake, muffins, Danish, and
cinnamon buns.

There are plenty of eggs and omelettes here too, as well as
pancakes and French toast. In addition to ordinary breakfast meats, pork roll is available.

Like most diners that have been able to remain successful
during this era of higher operating costs, the Burlington is a
family operation. The owners are proud that their children
are interested in the fine business they've built up, have the
same sense of pride in the quality of what's offered, and want
to continue with it.

There are many photos of famous sports figures displayed
behind the counter. Boxers, including Philadelphia's own Joe
Frazier, predominate. John told us that Joe DiMaggio once
stopped by for a meal and the diner was mobbed once word
got out that he was there.

An impressive selection of candy bars and tobacco goods
surrounds the counter by the cash register. In the hundreds
of diners we've visited, we've never seen anything to match
it.

*Taking a break*

# Big "E"

*Closter, New Jersey*

The Big "E" was brought up several years ago from its original location in Metuchen, New Jersey. We found this out from a little girl seated in the next booth who blurted out, "Daddy, is this the Duchess Diner?" Valerie, who along with her husband George, owns the Big "E," confirmed that it did indeed used to be the Duchess Diner before it was moved.

This has to be without a doubt the cleanest diner we have ever seen. George Foss prides himself on his handiness, and there's nothing in the Big "E" he hasn't worked on. He took us on a tour, showed us how he hand-tiled the luxurious rest rooms and put everything in the kitchen on wheels so that things could be moved for cleaning, and even pointed out how he had worked on the roof. To put it mildly, George was a little enthusiastic about everything he'd done. He even insisted on showing us the electrical wiring system and the sub-basement plumbing apparatus.

The inside of the Big "E," which is a late 1950s stainless steel Fodero diner, looks like a flying saucer. The pink-and-white recessed ceiling has a mirror running down the entire length of its center. If you stand in the middle of the diner and look up, the whole counter is reflected upside down. The counter top is cotton-candy pink, and the green terrazzo floor has touches of pink in it. The booths are green, while the walls and the base of the counter are pink and white. There are blue glass stripes worked into the stainless steel exterior. Everything inside is spotlessly clean and polished to a shine.

The food at the Big "E" is better than average, and there's a varied menu. Eggplant parmigiana with salad is about $2.50 and cheese blintzes with blueberry sauce are the same price. Corned beef, pastrami, and Reuben sandwiches are on the menu, and we found the meat to be quite good. We also tried the chicken, which was cooked with peppers and fresh tomato and served on a bed of rice, smothered in gravy. This dish will run you about $3.00. More standard diner fare, such as the knockwurst and sauerkraut with mashed potato or baked beans, is also on the menu, as well as eggs and omelettes.

Valerie is a woman who likes to enjoy herself, and you should come to this diner prepared. If you think that practical jokes have gone out of style, you are in for a surprise. When we tried to lift our cups to drink our coffee, we found that they were glued to the saucers. Valerie thought this was hilarious. Then, asking us if we liked to gamble, she brought out a toy one-armed bandit. The machine is fixed and always comes up three cherries; your "prize," however, is a stream of water that hits you squarely in the face. The machine takes a nickel, which she supplies. After we tried it once, she held up another nickel, asking us if we cared to try again. This was a trick coin, with a rubber back. When you squeeze the coin, as she did, it also squirts a stream of water into some unsuspecting victim's face. Valerie couldn't stop laughing.

*The Crystal Diner*

*Terry and friend*

## Crystal Diner

*Dumont, New Jersey*

Because of its hours, the Crystal is primarily a working-class diner. It's rare to find a tourist here, which is part of what appeals to us about the Crystal. Other pluses are the hearty food, the simple diner decor, and Terry Dogali, the owner.

Terry is a large blond woman who presides over her restaurant with a warm familiarity, although at first she was a little suspicious of us. Like many diner owners, she found it hard to believe that we were really interested in her diner, and she suspected us of being spies from McDonald's. When we finally convinced her otherwise, we got into a long conversation on the evils of fast food. Terry takes pride in her home cooking, and she resents what she sees as the impersonal cooking and service that fast-food restaurants offer. It must have been a full five minutes before she finished delineating the evils of these food chains. All the while, one of her regular customers sat patiently at the end of the counter, listening to the conversation and waiting to order. When Terry finally turned to him he asked, with a sly grin, for a "Big Mac."

Most of the customers we saw in the Crystal were town workers—police officers, sanitation crews, railroad men, construction workers, and the road crew. These patrons like their food simple and solid, and Terry doesn't disappoint them. One of her specials is something called a Hobo—

"Swap 2 Spies, Five Dissidents"

potatoes and eggs prepared German-style. The recipe was inherited from the previous owners. Charlie, a customer who runs the garage down the block, remembered eating this dish when the diner was new, over forty years ago. He also recalled seeing the diner brought into town and slid down skids onto its foundation—something we'd heard about often but were never lucky enough to see for ourselves.

Some other dishes that are available at the Crystal are the baked ziti, which sells for about $2.00, and the fillet of sole, which is priced slightly higher. The diner also makes its own soups: beef barley, chicken, and vegetable, for example. There is no printed menu, so check the wall where the specials are posted.

We couldn't determine the manufacturer of the Crystal Diner. The outside walls and been bricked over, although the barrel roof remains intact. Inside, the diner is predominantly green. Thre are green and blue mosaic tiles, and the white ceiling reflects the counter's green Formica marble swirl. It's a narrow diner with five booths. An antique hanging chandelier dominates the lighting space. The whole place has a decidedly 1950s feel, right down to the chrome ashtrays, even though the diner probably pre-dates that decade.

While you're at the Crystal, order something fried. The old Hotpoint deep-fryer bubbles with oil so loudly that it could serve as a model of a volcano on the *Mr. Wizard* TV show. The word HOTPOINT also lights up bright red when the machine is in operation.

John Aldridge

## White Manna

*Hackensack, New Jersey*

The White Manna was built in 1937 by Jerry O'Mahoney for one purpose, to act as a showplace diner at the 1939 World's Fair. It served only hamburgers and soda. There were originally four of these compact hamburger heavens built, but only one other remains. After the fair was over, the diner was moved to a less noble site overlooking the Hackensack River. It now resides on a strip populated by fast-food joints, gas stations, and auto supply stores that belie its halcyon days as the fairgrounds' queen of quick eating.

The owner of the White Manna is John C. Aldridge. A hardworking, soft-spoken man, John looks like veteran Western actor Ben Johnson. We thought he might have stepped right off the screen out of a John Ford film. John talked about the time he spends running his diner, but he wasn't complaining. It's all a matter of perspective. "Everybody talks about the good old days," he said. "They weren't so good to me. In 1935 I was working in a White Castle, from five pm till three am. After two years, working six days a week, I got a two-cents-an-hour raise." Today John is doing well, and all he sells are hamburgers—tiny ones, at that.

The diner, which is only sixteen feet wide, is a compact square of aluminum, glass brick, and tile. The base of the horseshoe-shaped counter is glass brick. The whole place is horseshoe-shaped. There's only enough room for sixteen people to sit at the counter, but John will sell five hundred burgers on a weekday and almost twice that many on a weekend. Of course, it's not hard to eat four of these White Castle–like burgers in a sitting, since they're as delicious as they are small.

The outside front wall of the diner is made from glass brick where the diner curves. Inside, the place is tiled in black, with some red and orange. The diner is kept so clean that the highly polished chrome cash register reflects the plastic ketchup and mustard dispensers, the salt and pepper shakers, and the napkin holder.

The night we were there, a local high school beauty named Janet was working the grill. Janet's ambition in life is to become a star, and if she does everything as well as she makes those burgers, her dream probably will come true. She can slice those burger rolls as fast as lightning, two at a time, and she has perfected the art of making White Manna burgers: taking a small ball of ground meat, flattening it with a spatula on the tiny grill that's right behind the counter, and cooking it in a pool of onion and juice from the meat. The aroma from the cooking of these quality burgers is so rich and strong you can smell it a block away.

Watching the burgers being made is half the fun. The waitresses are wired for action as these little slabs of meat come smashing down on the grill, five or six at a time, followed by quick sprinklings of salt, pepper, and onions. It's nothing to see fifteen or twenty hamburgers crowding the grill at one time. Local folklore has it that Tiny, who weighs over 350 pounds, will have twenty for supper on any given night.

Not only was Janet adroit behind the grill; she had also mastered the art of handling the customers, some of whom had come in that night after having a few, and almost all of whom

*Horseshoe-shaped counter with glass brick base*

appeared to have stopped by for the sole purpose of watching her work. Whenever one of these guys got on her case, she gave as good as she got, never missing a beat as she turned out those burgers.

The White Manna is the forerunner of the modern fast-food burger joint. But the difference in quality is so great that the newer ones seem almost a joke. Not only does John serve fresh meat, never frozen, but he also has buns baked especially for his burgers. And he personally spends one night each week, after closing, scrubbing every nook and cranny, to prevent any grease buildup.

John bought this diner in 1948 for $10,000. Today it would be impossible to replace. He had to move it once, about ten years ago, from an adjacent lot. The moving of this historical diner made all the local papers.

Some of the White Manna's customers have been coming there for thirty years or more. After watching the care that goes into every phase of John's operation, we're sure that White Manna is a candidate for diner heaven.

*Corner detail*

## Rosie's Farmland Diner

*Little Ferry, New Jersey*

*Rosie's Farmland Diner*

Almost everyone reading this book has seen Rosie's Farmland, even if you're not aware of it. This diner has been the scene of countless commercials, the most famous being the Bounty paper towel commercial, starring Nancy Walker as Rosie, who seems to have an endless stream of sloppy customers. In real life, the diner is owned by Ralph Corrado, who runs it with his son, Arnie.

Rosie's is a deluxe edition of a 1940s Paramount diner. It's so wide it had to be made in two sections, which were joined together lengthwise down the middle. A series of columns runs down the center of the diner, something we haven't come across anywhere else.

The filming of all the commercials has turned Ralph into something of a celebrity, and he could be mistaken for a movie producer but Ralph, who's as fine a gentleman as you'll ever meet, is a true dinerman at heart. His father owned a small Kullman diner in Hoboken—long gone now—and Ralph wishes he knew what became of it. He speaks fondly of the day they first brought the diner in from Kearny, New Jersey.

"I was about six years old. I'll never forget it. They let me stay up that night. We seen it from, like, five blocks away, coming down the middle of the street, because they brought it in the night. I'll never forget it."

*Gallery of stars*

Rosie's is basically the same as it was when first built in 1942, although the counter has been replaced and some of the colors were changed to accommodate the people who shot the commercials. There's lots of stainless steel and glass brick inside this enormous diner. The men's room sign, and some of the other decorative touches, shows a definite art-deco influence. There's also a jukebox, and Arnie, who's also a musician, has several of his own records on the machine.

Above the counter are photos of the many celebrities who have worked Rosie's Farmland doing commercials. There's also a huge aquarium full of tropical fish behind the counter.

Besides Ralph and Arnie, one of the regular workers is a fellow named Benny, who works behind the counter or waits on tables. Benny is always found wearing his whites and a soda-jerk hat with his name on it. He has the look of a man who knows diners.

At night, Ralph does all the cooking for the next day. The menu is fairly simple, the food is good, and the prices are reasonable, considering the diner is so close to New York City.

The goulash Ralph makes comes from an old German recipe, and it was one of our favorite dishes; the ingredients include beef, tomato juice, onions, paprika, Burgundy, and bay leaves. Not everything is prepared fresh—for instance, the honey-dipped fried chicken is frozen—but the quality of everything served is well maintained. Among the other specials are liver steak (a big seller), fish-and-chips, veal parmigiana, fillet of sole, fried scallops, shrimp, and fish cakes. And Ralph has two sandwiches on the menu that he named after his parents. He's that type of guy.

The daily special includes soup, entrée, two vegetables, and bread and butter. All the soups are made from scratch,

"Serving you, Benny"

and the list includes chicken rice, vegetable, beef, Yankee bean, and Manhattan-style clam chowder.

Because of all the commercials made in his diner—Sanka, Clorets, Pepsi, and Body-All are some—Ralph and Arnie have become major personalities in their own right. Customers frequently ask them to pose for pictures, and if they're not too busy they'll be happy to. But one drawback to the fame is that people are constantly stealing the menus, which cost five dollars apiece to replace, so please leave the menus there.

In spite of his fame, Ralph longs to be back in his dad's little old green Kullman. "I wish I was in that diner back then," he confided to us in his soft-spoken manner. However, we're glad he's right where he is. Rosie's Farmland is a treat. And please, try to resist asking for Rosie—she's not there anyway.

*Princeton, New Jersey*

The College Inn, which is also known as Pietrinferno's, is well known in Princeton for great burgers and Italian dishes. It's run by the Pietrinferno family, and Mrs. P does all the cooking herself.

This is a diner with a real homey feel. Mrs. P's mom used to run a boardinghouse, and she grew up learning how to cook for, and cater to, the public. "The very main thing with food is you must love what you're doing," she told us. "I'd never turn my kitchen over to a short-order cook. When I go home, the pot's on the stove, and I'll cook some more." We asked her young grandson, who was sitting at the next table, if it was true that she cooks so much. "Oh, yeah," he replied, "she cooks all the time."

One thing Mrs. P prepares is homemade minestrone soup. It's a real favorite with the local business people who lunch regularly at the diner. The coleslaw and potato salad are made on the premises, as well as the biscuits and corn muffins. Mrs. P explained why she does so much herself.

"You have to do this in business, especially small business like this. You have to do something for the public, you know. They like it.

"I don't advertise. You never see any of my advertisements in any papers. I put it on the plates. I really do. And nobody goes away hungry, never. If I think that they're still hungry, they get a little bit more."

One of our favorite sandwiches, which we make for ourselves at home, is tuna fish grilled with cheese and tomato. Before we went to the College Inn we had never seen this sandwich served in any restaurant, so we were pleasantly surprised to find it on the menu there. Other specialties include the homemade spaghetti sauce, plain or with meat, the baked ziti, and the cheese lasagna.

The burgers are seasoned according to a secret recipe that, as hard as we tried, we couldn't get Mrs. P to reveal. Two types of cheeseburgers that aren't commonly found on diner menus are offered: blue cheese and wine cheese. The wine cheese is a form of cheddar cheese spread, and extra seasoning is added to the cheese.

A real effort is made to serve dishes that people can afford, so you won't find thick steaks on the menu. You will find freshly made French vanilla pudding for dessert, and special holiday dishes: Easter cake, for example, at Easter. "It's just like a big home," Mrs. P told us. "When I think of something they'll like, I make it."

One of Princeton's big industries is Albert Einstein. Everyone has a story about the great man, but we couldn't prove that he actually ate at the College Inn. Someone who did eat there regularly, however, is Senator Bill Bradley, ex–New York Knickerbocker basketball player and former Princeton Rhodes Scholar. He's been eating there ever since his days as a student at Princeton. Of course, he's no longer a regular customer, but he does stop by whenever he's in town.

Besides cooking as though they were at home, the Petroinfernos keep the place as spotless as their own living room. We found the rest rooms quite clean, something we can't say about every diner we stopped at. For good food in pleasant surroundings, the College Inn rates high on our list.

## Bosko's Diner

*South River, New Jersey*

*Bosko's Diner*

When we first called Bosko on the phone and asked him if we could come out and talk with him, he was very reluctant. He told us that we didn't really want to talk to him, that his was just a small diner and what he could offer wouldn't be worth putting in a book. We were glad we didn't listen to him. Not only did we get a great meal and pleasant conversation, we got a lesson in diner history that we'll never forget.

Bosko has been in the diner business for close to fifty years. He started as a potato peeler and dishwasher while he was still in high school. In 1945, after he came out of the service, he went into business for himself, right where his diner is now. The current Bosko's Diner was bought in 1955 and is the last diner to come off the Jerry O'Mahony lot in Elizabeth, New Jersey. When Bosko bought the diner, O'Mahony had already declared bankruptcy and the building was parked on the street. It was put on huge wheels and hauled by tractor. Two days after it left Elizabeth, Bosko was in operation.

The Causeway, where the diner is located, was once the main highway. Now, after the construction of the turnpike, it's virtually a road to nowhere. Most of the customers are regulars, people Bosko has known all his life. Occasionally a trucker will come by, someone who remembers the diner from when it was on a trucker's route and who knows he can still get a good meal there.

*Bosko*

When we got to the diner, Bosko was seated in a booth, drinking coffee from a mug. A man in his mid-sixties with a shock of white hair and a long, creased face, he reminds us of Spencer Tracy. Dressed in white, he had a pack of Lucky Strikes in each breast pocket of his shirt. We commented on the metal awnings outside with B & T on them and asked if that was the true name of his diner. He informed us that it was a holdover from an earlier partnership and that these days the place is just called Bosko's.

Since it was Friday, and Bosko assured us that all his fish is cooked fresh—not frozen, never even put on the steam table—we had the fish dinner. Our mouths water as we recall the sweet flavor of that fried haddock. It was served with real mashed potatoes and the best coleslaw we've had in any diner. The secret of the coleslaw's flavor, we were told, is the ratio of vinegar to sugar. It was so good that, later that day when we stopped elsewhere for dinner and ordered coleslaw again, we felt insulted by the commercial slop they tried to pass off. The contrast was too great.

A fisherman's platter is offered every Friday. This consists of a fish cake, fried shrimp, scallops, and a piece of haddock. Served with potato, vegetable, and salad, it costs about $4.00. Fried oysters are another Friday special, and they sell out very quickly. Bosko double-breads his oysters—first with flour, then with cracker meal—so they puff up while frying. During Lent, he serves fish on Wednesdays.

Other specials include stuffed pork chops, roast beef, steak and peppers, stuffed cabbage, and turkey. Everything is fresh. Bosko makes corned beef, beef stew, and kidney stew. He'll buy a thirty-six-pound turkey, roast the breast, boil the remainder to make turkey salad and croquettes, and use the stock for soup. Using everything and wasting nothing is the secret of good fresh cooking.

Bosko told us many stories about the early days of diners and about life in South River, which is only a mile square. He told us about a tree-sitter he fed back in the 1930s. This fellow earned his living by traveling from town to town, finding a nice tall tree and sitting in the top of it for days. Today he'd probably be arrested immediately. We also heard about a twelve-hour marathon bike race that went around the diner and that Bosko himself participated in.

But what interested us most was the way Bosko talked about his early days in diners, and especially Boisey's Diner, where he learned his trade. He talked about working twelve hours a day seven days a week, and how it took him a year to work his way up from dishwasher to grillman. He still has a lot of reverence and respect for the owner of Boisey's, a pioneer dinerman in the 1920s who taught Bosko all he knew.

Diners, to Bosko, are as much a way of life as a business. He was a school kid when he started, and the diner world was a man's world. You would never see a woman in a diner. He's not sure why, but he thinks it might have something to do with the fact that there were no booths in the early diners, only stools, and this was before women wore slacks. The diner might have been a place where you'd hear plenty of rough language, but it was also a place where if you were down and out you could get a free meal. Meal tickets were also sold back in those days. No one had much money, and a working man was likely to spend his paycheck before he got his next one, so he'd buy a couple of meal tickets at once to know he'd have them and be able to exchange them for dinner at any time.

Bosko still sees the diner as a service institution, and his customers appreciate it. One fellow saw us talking to him and came over to tell us that Bosko is "Mr. Senior Citizen, and a good friend of the VFW"

*Alfrieda: she's worked with Bosko since 1955*

*Williamstown, New Jersey*

═══════════════════════

The Williamstown Diner is right off the Atlantic City Expressway, so if you're going to gamble, stop there for a sure thing and try some of the cherry cheesecake. The large, 1960s Mountain View diner has a big neon sign outside that's left over from when there used to be an older diner on the same spot. The sign reads BROASTED CHICKEN. Whatever type of chicken that may be, it remains a mystery to those who work at the diner now.

The building is a fairly large one, with a lot of white and yellow inside, a mirrored stripe running down the center of the ceiling, and bright-red booths. The rest rooms at this diner are also large, if not as clean as the dining area.

If you visit Steve and Nick's place (they're the owners) at five in the afternoon, you may be lucky enough to see Pop, a regular customer. Pop is in his early eighties and a former vaudevillian. He goes through his acts at the counter, telling jokes, singing songs, and getting up to do his dance routines. Pop calls all the waitresses "Mabel," no matter what their real names might be.

The girls behind the counter seem to have been selected from the local high school beauties—their average age: sixteen. When they saw us taking notes, they wanted to know if we were writing a "report." We felt as if we were back in ninth-grade social studies.

All the cooking is done in the kitchen, as this diner post-dates the era when grills were built up front. This is something we always regret, since watching a grillman at work is part of the diner experience.

The Williamstown advertises home-style cooking. We had the red snapper soup, which was very flavorful and slightly spicy. We also enjoyed the rigatoni with Italian sausage, and the meat lasagna was nicely flavored with garlic, basil, and bay leaves. On Sundays there is a chicken dumpling special.

Because this diner is in southern New Jersey, fish is popular. We had the homemade deviled clams, and they were very good. Deviled crab is also available. Other seafood specialties include fried oysters, broiled scallops, and bluefish. The coleslaw and potato salad are both homemade and well worth trying.

All the desserts are made on the premises. The cherry cheesecake is quite good, if a little on the sweet side; the rice pudding is tasty too. Complete fountain service is available.

Because this is a twenty-four-hour diner, it is a convenient place to stop both going to and coming home from the Jersey shore. While most of the customers are regulars, there is a large summer tourist trade.

## *Irene's Windsor Diner*

*Windsor, New Jersey*

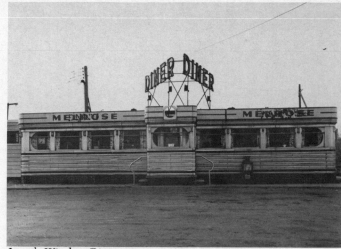

*Irene's Windsor Diner*

Central rural New Jersey is Anywhere, U.S.A. When we pulled into the parking lot in front of Irene's Windsor, there were several big semis parked there, as well as a jeep belonging to one of the local farmers. Suddenly the engine of the jeep burst into flames. One of the truck drivers rushed from the diner, took a fire extinguisher from the cab of his truck, and doused the flames. Welcome to the world of truck stops.

Irene's is a transitional diner built by O'Mahony in the early 1940s. Its exterior is pre–stainless steel, with art-deco yellow and green piping. The window in the entranceway looks like a giant porthole, and there's a half-moon-shaped window at each end of the building. The original name, Melrose Diner, still stands along the roof, a remnant from the days when this diner dinosaur was located in Philadelphia. Irene, who's owned the place since 1977, was told that it was moved to its present location twenty years ago.

Irene runs the diner with her family, but this frail blond woman does most of the work. Irene told us she had been a waitress most of her life and had always dreamed of owning her own diner. Since it's open twenty-four hours a day, her husband, Bob, works the night shift. There's a lot of work involved in making this dream come true.

The food is pretty simple at Irene's, and it's all home cooking. Breakfast is a big meal with the truckers, some of

*Irene*

whom are known to eat enormous portions. Four eggs with bacon and sausage, home fries, and a double order of toast is not unheard-of. Irene says there's one fellow who comes in and orders six eggs, but that's stretching a point.

Everything—except roasts, of course—is made to order. Meat loaf and roast beef are two of the daily specials. Hamburger steak and pork roll made from Taylor ham are other popular items. Irene's homemade bean soups are always in great demand. Actually, it's Bob who makes the soups. Navy bean, lima bean, Yankee bean, or any other type of bean soup is appreciated by the trucker clientele. The homemade chili is popular too.

In the summertime, Irene mostly uses fresh vegetables. Native tomatoes and local lettuce are always served. The potatoes are grown in New Jersey, and she'll buy any other fresh produce that's available. There was one item on the menu we had never heard of before—a "Beef Bopper." It turned out to be a hamburger patty made with green pepper and onion mixed into the meat, and like everything else in this diner it was reasonably priced. A full dinner at Irene's would cost you less than $3.00, although prices do fluctuate with costs.

Irene's Windsor is kept clean, but it shows the wear and tear of almost forty years of use. However, there are some touches inside that we rarely see in diners these days, like the silver chevrons inlaid in the tabletops, and the green racing stripe that's set into the counter top, running its entire length. The ceiling has riveted Formica panels, representative of what O'Mahony was doing in this transitional design period between the trolley-car style and the stainless steel look. A few of the lamps that are mounted on the wall along the booths still have their original milk glass shades. We

*Irene's daughter*

couldn't determine whether the different-colored stools were part of the original decor or had just been replaced one by one over the years.

In addition to serving her customers food, Irene provides a jukebox that specializes in country and western music, a pinball machine, a counter full of tobacco products that range from snuff to cigars, sunglasses, candies, costume jewelry, souvenir trinkets, a condom machine in the bathroom, and a TV set on the counter. The TV is one of the small portable Japanese models that can run on batteries or plug into the cigarette lighter in the car. It could be the most important item in the diner. Irene talked to us about the TV.

"A lot of the truck drivers like that. They can come in here and sit and watch TV. In the daytime I do most of the cooking. When I had a waitress out front we'd have two TVs. I had that one out in the kitchen and another one out here, and we'd put the stories on, and I'd watch my stories. We'd have the one back there and the one out here so we wouldn't miss it.

"I got one old guy comes in, and if it's not on he'll say, 'How come you don't have *The Young and the Restless* on?' He asks for it by name.

"My son works three to eleven, my redhead, and he's strictly hockey. At night that's all you got on that TV is hockey or the ball games. And the guys, the steady ones, or even the drivers, they'll sit and watch."

Irene's gets New York and Philadelphia stations, so for sports it's the Knicks, Rangers, Flyers, 76ers, Mets, Phillies, Yankees, Jets, Giants, and Eagles.

Irene's is a place where you get your atmosphere uncut and undiluted. When we first saw Irene, with her large, deep-set eyes, we thought of photographer Walker Evans's WPA portraits of migrant workers, but there's nothing sad about Irene. She loves her work and she loves dealing with her customers. If we ever put together a panel of great diner owners, Irene'll be right up there on the podium. Maybe it'll even be on TV.

*New York*

Lake George •

• North Syracuse

Schenectady •
Colonie •

• Polksville

• Binghamton          West Taghkanic •

Kingston •

• Monticello

Katonah •

Harrison •

New York          Astoria, Queens
                  •
          • Center Moriches

Brooklyn

*Astoria, Queens, New York*

Located close to La Guardia Airport, the Airline is a classic example of streamlined 1950s-style chrome-and-glass diner architecture. Visible from the main highway, especially at night when the neon sign flashes a series of revolving airplanes, the Airline Diner is a landmark for many travelers coming into New York. But besides these travelers and the occasional celebrities (Jackie Onassis and her chauffeur are known to grab a bite here on their way from the airport), the Airline is basically a family restaurant.

Stanley Koutsouradis, the diner's owner since 1970, takes great pride not only in the quality of the food served but also in the cleanliness of his establishment. And well he should, for the place sparkles. With its pink and green tiled walls, sleek Formica counter, and stainless steel stools, the diner looks just as it did when first built.

The Airline has a large selection of food with a full-sized menu and three different specials daily that cost about $3.00. The Yankee pot roast, with a rich brown gravy, is accompanied by a large potato pancake. All the daily specials come with a choice of two vegetables, salad, bread and butter, and coffee or tea. Another special, the Greek-style peppers stuffed with meat and rice, prepared in Stanley's own lemon and egg-based sauce, is a delight to eat. Friday is fish day, and one of the specials is shrimp scampi. The shrimp are served in a moderately spicy garlic sauce on a bed of rice. We found it quite tasty.

Stanley buys his vegetables fresh every week, personally going to the market to select them. He also buys his meat fresh and in bulk, carving it himself to guarantee quality. One of the regular items on the menu is the Greek salad— feta cheese, sardines, and tomatoes on a lettuce base—which makes a delicious light meal. At less than $3.00, it's also reasonable. There are "hefty hand-carved sandwiches" on the menu, and for under $2.00 you can have turkey, pastrami, or roast beef. They all make for good eating.

All dishes offered are available twenty-four hours a day. Whether you come in at 5:00 A.M. or 5:00 P.M., you can order breakfast, lunch, or dinner. Weekends draw a late-night crowd, with couples coming in after the local Queens discos close for the night, and it's not uncommon to see the counter filled at 3:00 A.M. on a Sunday.

Breakfast specials are served at the Airline from 6:00 A.M. to 11:00 A.M. Two eggs with toast, potatoes, and coffee cost $1.10; for only 40 cents more you can have bacon, ham, or sausage, making this one of New York City's better breakfast buys. Stanley bakes his own breakfast muffins, although all the other breads and cakes are baked for him. He also serves an excellent cup of coffee, something that seems harder and harder to come by these days.

Like most quality diner owners, Stanley is warm, generous, and hardworking. He gets great satisfaction from watching his patrons enjoy themselves and seems pleasantly surprised at the attention the Airline has been receiving. Several advertising agencies have shot commercials there, and one feature film used the diner for a location. The film company offered Stanley one thousand dollars if he would close half a day for them. He told them no. They could film there, he said, but only in part of his diner. His customers come first. The food and the service always reflect this attitude.

## Danny's Diner

*Binghamton, New York*

Danny's Diner is located right next to the small arch that marks the Binghamton–Johnson City border. These twin cities are something right out of a Raymond Chandler novel. They reminded us of what Philip Marlowe, Chandler's fictional detective, must have found in Bay City—especially Johnson City, where we could easily imagine gambling tables in the basement of one of the local eateries. But we liked Danny's Diner, and we particularly liked Danny Giannichi's wife, Sharon, who waited on the hungry and demanding customers with grace and ease. Sharon complained to us that everyone remembers her husband's name but forgets her name, referring to her as "Danny's wife." So we'll repeat it three times: Sharon, Sharon, Sharon.

Danny's is a 1940s Silk City diner that shows some signs of wear and has had some minor remodeling but is basically in its original condition. We were pleased to find a Silk City of that vintage, still in such good shape, in New York State.

There's a good mix of students and local folks at Danny's, since Harpur College is in Binghamton.

The peak hours are 11:30 A.M. to 2:00 P.M., and the scene is not unlike feeding time at the zoo. These people are hungry, and they want their food *now*. We watched Sharon zipping down the serving corridor, clearing tables with one hand, delivering orders with the other. We were impressed with her skill, but Sharon is pretty blasé about it all. Not surprising, since she's been at it so long.

The diner used to have a glass counter, but the top has been replaced with Formica. While new booths have been added, the original oak trim is still visible around the windows. The barreled ceiling, with its wood striping, is still intact. There is a new linoleum floor, and one of the original seats from the first booths, a horseshoe-shaped affair, remains at the rear of the diner.

The menu at Danny's is fairly extensive and moderately priced. Five different specials are listed each day on a blackboard. Every Thursday it's chicken and biscuits. (We found the gravy heavy and the meat scarce.) Sharon told us that they didn't serve it one Thursday and everyone complained. Friday is macaroni-and-cheese day. Other specials are the beef barbecue on a bun and creamed chipped beef.

Sharon told us that much of her stamina dates back to the days she and her husband first took over the diner. She used to be very shy, and diner customers everywhere are notorious for the insults they like to fling over the counter. She'd spent hours weeping out back until one day Danny told her to dish the dirt out in return. She discovered that it worked, and a new woman was born.

Danny and Sharon take good care of their regulars. One fellow—who is now confined to a wheelchair, lives in a nursing home, and suffers mild mental lapses—still comes in daily. The management lets him sit as long as he likes and calls a cab for him to get home when he's ready.

Sharon told us that she likes the idea of having the grill up front. It gives her a sense of community and enables her to see what's going on at all times. Besides, Danny is a virtuoso with hotcakes and eggs, and that provides entertainment for customers who are waiting for their breakfast.

*Brooklyn, New York*

═══════════════════════════════

Yes, Virginia, there is a real silver diner left in Brooklyn. We thought they had all been replaced by the new Greco-Roman monstrosities, but then we remembered the Blue Bird back in the old neighborhood, and it's as bright and clean and shiny as ever.

We took a tour of Brooklyn with an octogenarian friend of ours, Izzy Snow. After reminding us of the Blue Bird, Izzy took us around the borough to point out other diners that he remembered from his days as a pastry-truck driver. We found four of them, but only one, Toomy's, which sits across from the site of the old Ebbets Field, still functions as a diner. One of the others, a gorgeous yellow-enameled Silk City from the 1930s, is now the office of a construction company. Of the other two, one sits boarded up in the Williamsburg section, and the other, recognizable as a diner only by its barreled roof, is a tire repair shop on Fourth Avenue. Only the Blue Bird, which is located one block from Kings Highway at the corner of Utica Avenue, has kept its original splendor.

The Blue Bird, a twenty-four-hour diner, was built about thirty years ago by Silk City, a division of the Patterson Vehicle Company. There are six blue booths inside, with one large horseshoe-shaped booth at the end. The stools are blue, and blue-lace curtains hang at all the windows. Blue trim runs between the windows and the white-enamel ceiling.

The floor is brown and blue mosaic; the tabletops and counter tops are white Formica with a blue marbled pattern. There is stainless steel all along the wall behind the counter area, and the outside of the diner is all stainless steel, with blue-enamel stripes that run horizontally. It's not for nothing that the place is called the Blue Bird.

The food at the Blue Bird is classic diner fare, and the prices, for New York City, are quite reasonable. Several daily specials, such as corned beef and cabbage and pepper steak with rice, are offered. Both of those dishes go for about $3.50. Baked macaroni, another daily special, will run you about $2.00. Southern fried chicken and broiled pork chops also appear on the menu.

A breakfast special—eggs, juice, home fries, toast, and coffee—is served for $1.10 until 11:00 A.M. After that time no more home fries are served, only french fries. The Blue Bird is one of the very few diners we found that makes its own french fries from whole potatoes. Almost all restaurants use frozen fries these days.

Puddings, such as rice pudding, are made on the premises, as are the corn and bran muffins. Most of the soups are made from scratch, and hamburger patties are formed by hand. This is a real diner in the old tradition. Many of the grillmen have been there for years, and you get that timeless feeling of being in any diner, at any time, when you sit at the counter here.

The place is kept immaculate. Between shifts everything is washed down, including the walls, and the ceiling is cleaned with ammonia once or twice a month. A lot of care is put into the running of this diner, and its patrons appreciate that. There are several more modern so-called diners in the area, but the customers of the Blue Bird remain loyal. It has the usual diner clientele: city workers, cops, hoods, factory workers, and neighborhood people. On weekend nights especially, the place is jumping. Couples come in after the movies or a night at the discos, and single men come in to sober up after the bars close.

Recently, a newsstand has been built onto the diner. Called Frank's, it sells all the local papers, as well as candy, cigarettes, playing cards, magazines, and anything else a newsstand might carry. So if you want to relax, stop at Frank's for the paper, then go inside for fast service, a leisurely meal, and pleasant company at Brooklyn's last true diner.

*Center Moriches, New York*

Duffy's is a 1920s diner of indeterminate origin. Built before booths became standard diner equipment, three tables were added when several of the stools were removed. Otherwise, you'll dine at the counter of this rustic lunch wagon.

Most of the customers at Duffy's are regulars—old-timers—and charter fishermen coming in for breakfast, many of whom come out on boats from Sheepshead Bay, Brooklyn. Gladys Duffy, who owns Duffy's, has only been running it for the last three years. She had lots of experience working as a waitress before she decided to become a diner owner.

Gladys and her husband own a boat that's docked at this waterfront town, and they used to stop by the diner regularly. When they heard it was up for sale, they decided to give it a whirl. Like all diner owners, Gladys finds it's a lot of work, but she enjoys it.

The reason this diner's origins are shrouded in mystery is that so much has been done to change its looks. Sheet metal adorns the outside, and while some parts of the inside walls sport wood paneling, the rest has been covered with yellow and gold wallpaper. The wall that runs below the window has been tiled over in a multicolored mosaic. The original barreled ceiling remains, however.

Gladys offers different daily specials and keeps the menu simple. Three of her staples are meat loaf, roast beef, and ham roast. These come with potato, vegetable, bread and butter, and coffee. The average price for the daily special is about $3.25.

The diner is famous for its sandwiches, which are huge. There is a selection of hot and cold sandwich meats. A hot open-face sandwich special, which comes with potato and coleslaw, runs about a dollar less than the platters.

The mashed potatoes are instant, and the coleslaw is commercial, although it's very good. This is the way that food has been served at Duffy's for years, since way before Gladys took over, and it's what satisfies the regulars who keep coming back.

You might think that because this diner caters to so many fishermen, fresh fish would be served. Wrong. But there is an excellent homemade red fish chowder, and all the soups are made from scratch.

Gladys is secretary of the local chamber of commerce and takes a strong interest in the community. She posts information about, and results of, the local fishing tournaments as well as other sporting events. Gladys told us that when the film *Jaws* came out, Center Moriches was full of fishermen looking for the great white shark. Although shark fever has died down somewhat, shark fishing remains a popular sport.

The beaches in this town are open in the summer, and it's a nice place to visit if you're looking to get away from it all on those hot summer weekends. As Duffy's is on the way to Montauk and the Hamptons, it is an ideal stopping place for a late-morning vacation breakfast.

## *Charlie's Northway Diner*

*Colonie, New York*

Charlie's Northway is one of the most modern diners listed in this guide. It's a late-vintage Silk City, with no grill (all the food is prepared in the kitchen) and with huge windows all the way around the front. If you get a chance, compare this diner to an earlier Silk City, like the Blue Benn in Bennington, Vermont. The manufacturer maintained many of the original design concepts but modified them so that they are more in tune with modern styling and materials. This diner is a far cry from its older cousins, but the family resemblance is definitely there.

Charlie's Northway is primarily a trucker's stop. Breakfast specials are offered from 5:00 A.M. to 10:00 A.M. Pancakes cost $1.10, and blueberry pancakes are 60 cents more. Home fries are extra with your eggs.

The rest of the menu is fairly extensive. The average price for a dinner is about $3.50. Some of the specials listed include pot roast, pork chops, fried scallops, and baked meat loaf. All dinners come with hot rolls or bread, potato, vegetable, and salad. There are plenty of sandwiches, as well as five different types of club sandwiches: turkey, roast beef, ham, chicken salad, and tuna.

We spoke with the cashier, a Mrs. Peterson, who told us that prior to working in the diner she had spent fifteen years in a state office building. When asked how her present job compared to her old one, she cleared her throat and said, in a very sincere tone of voice, that the truckers were quite different from the people she used to work with, especially if the service was too slow. Since she had started working there, however, she had become quite fond of "the boys" and was particularly touched by the feeling of comradery and the concern that's shown should one of them be involved in an accident. The day we were there, a truck had jackknifed on the thruway, and everyone was talking about what they could do to help out. There was a real sense that traffic accidents are a job hazard no trucker is immune to and that everyone must work together in the face of such a disaster.

We found waitresses and customers alike to be quite friendly. When we asked for directions, the whole diner chipped in. Charlie's is located right alongside the beginning of the Northway (Interstate 87), just above Albany. So if you're headed up to the Adirondacks, stop by and tank up with some of Charlie's fine coffee and sandwiches.

*Harrison, New York*

Here's a diner where you can get not only Chinese food but also home-style Chinese cooking. The Chinatown Diner, known as Cappy's in its pre-oriental days, is run by the Pea family. George Pea supervises in the evenings, greeting customers and taking orders, while his parents oversee the kitchen. During the day, George's sister Alice runs the diner.

All food at the Chinatown is prepared to order, made with fresh ingredients and *without* MSG. Vegetarian dishes are a specialty at the Chinatown, and all selections are truly excellent. We've never eaten Chinese food of such high quality outside New York City's Chinatown. The only drawback was the grease in the diner. Wok cooking (and it's all wok cooking) creates a lot of smoke. Charles Green, a longtime Harrison resident who remembers Cappy's, recalls it as a greasy diner. So maybe it's the smoke, or maybe it's just tradition, but it is something you'll have to deal with if you eat at the Chinatown. However, in all fairness, we must tell you that we didn't find it so greasy that we haven't gone back many times to enjoy the delicious cooking.

The Chinatown is a pink diner of unknown origin, about thirty years old. We guess it was built by the Kullman people. The building itself is basically intact, although the booths have been removed and replaced with tables. A few pictures and calendars depicting oriental scenes hang inside, possibly to meet the expectations of occidental patrons.

Most of the customers at the Chinatown are regulars, and they all greet George with a friendly hello. Like his more traditional diner counterparts, George finds pleasure in serving all kinds of people. "We get any kind of class. Any kind of people," he told us. "Because if you have good food and a good price, then you can service any kind of customers. Kids, young fellows, the working class. You know. Any kind of people."

Good food at good prices is the story at the Chinatown. The portions are enormous and very cheap. A family of four can eat well and pay no more than twenty dollars tops. The Pea family had a restaurant in Taiwan before coming to America, and Mrs. Pea cooks all the dishes to order in the high-ceilinged kitchen the same way she's been doing it for forty years.

We were puzzled by the term "home-style" Chinese cooking, but it all became clear to us once the food was served. There's nothing commercial about this fresh food. Besides the excellent taste, another by-product of the freshness is the bright color of the crisp vegetables. The greens, reds, yellows, and oranges all jump out at you from the plate, almost as if some artist had created these platters on canvas. Every Sunday the whole Pea family goes down to New York's Chinese district to shop, because that's the only place they can find the fresh ingredients they need.

Vegetable-and-rice dishes are a big item at this restaurant. They are made with rice, parsley, bean sprouts, bean curd, water chestnuts, bamboo shoots, carrots, onions, mushrooms, and a few other ingredients. A rice dish can be ordered plain or with roast pork, shrimp, or chicken. There is also a bean-curd rice that contains enormous chunks of that mild, white soybean product.

Other dishes we found interesting at this Mandarin-style Chinese restaurant were pepper steak, Moo Goo Gai Pan (chicken with mushrooms), spareribs (neither too sweet nor too sticky), and Egg Fu Yung. Most restaurants prepare their fu yung pancake-style, but Mrs. Pea mixes her vegetables and other ingredients together with the eggs, scrambling it all in the wok. She then covers everything with rice and butter. We loved it.

There are a number of lo mein, or noodle, and chow mein dishes. And there's something called Chicken Wing Ding that you should ask about. Like everything else, the egg rolls are made fresh. For soup, we recommend the hot and sour—it's chockful of egg and vegetables, as well as seasoning.

The Chinatown provides an American breakfast that's priced very reasonably. Since the diner is located directly across the street from the Harrison train station, many commuters stop in for pancakes and coffee, or bacon and eggs, on their way to work.

The entire Pea family is warm and friendly, even though the elder Peas speak no English. When we told George we wanted to compliment his folks on their fine cooking, he brought them out from the kitchen. As he translated our praise, they bowed their appreciation to us in the old-world way.

The diner is closed Sundays and gets very busy on Friday and Saturday nights. Since it closes at 9:00 P.M., we recommend that you come early if you wish to eat there on a weekend.

## Blue Dolphin Diner

*Katonah, New York*

*The chef at work in the Blue Dolphin's kitchen*

Unfortunately, the Blue Dolphin has had a face-lift since we were first there. The original barrel–topped roof of this forty-year-old Kullman diner has been replaced by a fake mansard roof that covers almost the entire front of the building. Nevertheless, fellow diner lovers, we heartily recommend the Blue Dolphin as a true diner and a haven of peace and tranquility that's sure to promote good digestion.

Katonah is an attractive town, a quiet town, and a dry town. Every year there's an effort to legalize the sale of liquor in this downstate community, and every time legalization appears on the ballot the townspeople vote against it. This is the only dry town we've heard of in New York State.

The Blue Dolphin sits on a hill in the center of Katonah. The view from the booth windows is of small shops and the old train station. The diner itself serves as a meeting place for many of the older town residents. The owner discourages the local kids from hanging out—he had the jukebox removed—and he enjoys having a calm diner. The food is of high quality, and the kitchen is immaculate.

Everything served in the Blue Dolphin is prepared fresh, including the desserts. The regular menu is large and well-balanced, with very reasonable prices. It features cold buffet platters such as egg, chicken, or shrimp salad served on a bed of lettuce with homemade potato salad, coleslaw, and sliced tomato and cucumber. Dietetic dishes are available, mainly fruit or salads served with cottage cheese. There are also special salads, like the chef's salad or the Greek salad, which is made with feta cheese (a Greek goat cheese), anchovies, lettuce, tomato, and cucumber.

Sandwiches are a popular item at the Blue Dolphin. Offerings include club sandwiches served with a side of potato salad; a Monte Cristo (sliced turkey, ham, and melted Swiss cheese served on French toast); and a Reuben sandwich (corned beef, sauerkraut, and melted Swiss cheese). Every day at lunchtime a sandwich special is available. One time we were there it was a chicken salad sandwich served with french fries, beef barley soup that had chunks of beef floating in generous proportions, rice puddings or Jell-O, and coffee—all for $2.00.

In addition to salads, soups, and sandwiches, Italian dishes, entrées, and roasts, and seafood are regular items. Baked sausages, a small shell steak, breaded veal cutlet, and veal parmigiana are all available daily. The seafood is broiled fresh halibut in butter sauce, fried shrimp, fillet of sole, or scallops—all served with potato, vegetable, and tossed salad. The Italian plates are spaghetti or ravioli, served with meatballs or marinara sauce.

Three different specials are added to the menu daily. One special that we found particularly pleasing was the braised lamb shank. The lamb was served in a sauce made from its own juices and topped with cooked tomato and onion. The fresh potato salad was an excellent side dish for this platter. We also found the stuffed peppers to be quite good.

Although the portions were not enormous, we felt very satisfied when we left the table, especially after we had some of the Blue Dolphin's fabulous homemade cheesecake. In addition to the cheesecake, which is made from cottage cheese, the homemade rice pudding, which has a distinctive taste, was as good as we've had in any diner.

There is a full breakfast menu, of course, and bagels are available for those who want more than just toast. The Blue Dolphin does have a soda fountain, something that's not too common in diners. Egg creams, malteds, and ice-cream sodas can be sipped in comfort at the counter or in the booths.

Most of the customers here are regulars, and the atmosphere is friendly and chatty. We got involved in an engrossing conversation on the state of numismatics in America with one white-haired gentleman at the counter. He discoursed with great passion on the subject, and we, as strangers, appreciated his brief company while we were on the diner trail.

## *Colonial Diner*

*Kingston, New York*

The Colonial is a shiny Silk City diner, built in the late 1940s and owned by a husband-and-wife team, Gene and Litza Zachariou, who deserve a lot of credit for keeping the diner in perfect condition without remodeling. The Colonial, which is set at a right angle to the street, is a pleasure to see, especially at night when the lights out front highlight its enamel exterior. The neon DINER sign is a festival of blue, green, and red and beckons to you to come on in.

The interior of the Colonial is also a visual treat. The ceiling is an ivory-colored enamel, and the walls are a combination of stainless steel and wood, the wooden part being the frames around the windows. The wooden booths are upholstered in a turquoise shade, the floors are brown tile, and the base of the counter is tiled in black and white. Somehow all this works together, and sitting in the diner, whether in a booth or at the counter, is a comfortable experience.

Litza and Gene are a study in contrasts. We were impressed with Litza's skill as a waitress. She handled the whole floor with ease and confidence, and the place was packed. She could keep six orders in her head while five others were going out and show no signs of being flustered. While she ran back and forth and called orders out to Gene, who works behind the counter, he remained placid, almost unmoving. When we commented on the difference in their styles, Litza remarked, "I lose weight, he gains weight."

The food at the Colonial is quite good, and roasts are a specialty of the house. The chili is homemade (about $1.25 for a bowl and a hard roll), and there is a hooded charcoal broiler where steaks, chops, and burgers are cooked. In addition to the large grill out front, there's an enormous deep-fryer that was turning out fried fish and potatoes the entire time we were there. All portions were enormous; we were unable to finish our steak dinner, which is a rare occurrence indeed.

The Colonial is big on hot sandwiches. An open-face meatball sandwich with a side of potatoes costs $1.65. *Souvlaki* and pastrami with melted cheese on rye are on the menu at all times.

We were very pleased with our soup, which was clam chowder and came in a tremendous bowl. A cup of soup at the Colonial is the same size as a bowl at other restaurants, and the bowl is almost a meal in itself. The chowder was seasoned with basil and oregano and tasted as good as any that we've had in New York City's Little Italy.

While we were eating, I noticed that Litza took an order for dinner over the phone, mentioning a time—"eight o'clock." At precisely eight o'clock she served dinner for four to an empty booth, and immediately afterward four women came into the diner, sat down at the table, and began eating. We asked Litza if it was common for people to order over the phone like that. She told us that sometimes when people were working and didn't have much time to eat, she'd help them out this way.

While we were having dessert at the counter—a mediocre blueberry pie that was baked at the diner and had thick filling from a can—we struck up a conversation with a couple who were obviously enjoying their dinner. He was Gerry Hilly, a lawyer for Vincent Sardi, the famous restaurateur, and she taught home economics in high school and seemed to be a real food expert. They told us that they always eat in diners when they're on the road (they had stopped off in Kingston on their way to Vermont) and that they prefer the old diners and will go out of their way to find one, because they can always depend on consistent quality. The lawyer told us that even when he's traveling with Sardi they often choose to eat in a true diner. When we showed them a copy of Baeder's book of diner paintings they became quite enthused, and we all began talking about our favorite diners. They showed the book to a few of the local kids who were seated next to them, but the kids just stared blankly at the pictures. Maybe they were wondering where the McDonald's was.

## Prospect Mountain Diner

*Lake George, New York*

Ever since the Prospect Mountain Diner was written up in *New York Magazine*, the place hasn't had a moment's rest. Besides being a twenty-four-hour diner seven days a week, this stainless steel Silk City diner is unusual in that it serves Chinese food, in the diner itself and an adjoining dining room, the Rickshaw Annex.

The first things you notice inside the diner are the chrome-plated ceiling fans (not part of the original design), the sleek deco wall boards, and the red-leather booths.

Art Leonard, the owner, dims the lights in the diner after midnight as a service to his customers, many of whom are couples who have just met each other at a local nightclub. He wants to put off until sunrise the surprise they might experience by getting a good look at each other. A true dinerman, Art went into hock to start this place. Through hard work, excellent food and service, and a reputation for having a clean diner, he now can afford to own two other restaurants in town.

The food is outstanding and unusually diversified for a diner, Art having employed the same chef for the last seven years. Regular diner fare is also available in the dining room.

You'll find plenty of omelettes on the menu, as well as a steak-and-egg platter that comes with three eggs. Omelettes include fresh mushroom, Western, farmer's (potato, ham, sausage, peppers, and onions; an Adirondack specialty), pizza, and egg foo yung. There are egg specials, like eggs Benedict and shirred eggs en casserole. And this is one of the few diners that serve waffles: plain or pecan, with strawberries, blueberries, or ice cream.

Dinner specials include chicken dumplings served over homemade biscuits with gravy and sausage, trout cooked in butter and lemon, and Art's own smoked pork sausages, which are famous all over town.

There is a huge sandwich selection, which includes several hot sandwiches and a classic triple-decker.

The Prospect Mountain gets lots of truckers and tourist buses because it has ample parking and quick service. On the CB scanner behind the counter, frequently late at night, a waitress will hear one traveler recommend the diner to another. And sometimes the local police will answer a call over the radio for a good place to eat.

Lake George is a well-known resort town, and a ride along the Northway is a trip along one of America's most beautiful highways. If you're up that way, you should definitely make this diner a part of your trip. Just imagine, skillet steak served in the skillet or on a platter, cooked Chinese style with pepper and onions, or Welsh rarebit en casserole, or egg roll, or spareribs Cantonese-style, or pork chops with applesauce. We get hungry just remembering this menu. Many a trucker comes off the Northway, passes up everything on "the strip," and pulls into the Prospect Mountain for a great meal. We'd follow these truckers, if we were you.

## *Marybill Diner*

*Merrick, New York*

Most of the older diners on Long Island have been remodeled, Mediterraneanized to death. So it was a pleasure to find a vintage 1949 Silk City diner in mint condition. It's owned by Mary and Nick Kolkos, who bought it from Mary's parents, who in turn bought it from the original Mary and Bill, lifelong friends of theirs (the original Mary was the current owner's godmother). This is truly a neighborhood restaurant.

Mary had been working as a secretary in Manhattan, and Nick, who came from Greece in 1970, was working as a dental technician, when the diner was put up for sale. Mary, who had spent many summers and weekends working there, couldn't bear to see the place sold to strangers, so she decided she and Nick should take it over. She hasn't regretted it for a moment.

The inside of this diner is a treat to see, much more so than a glance at the outside might suggest. The Silk City people designed their barreled ceilings so they slanted down at both ends, giving the full effect of a train car. Other trainlike characteristics include the sliding doors, which, like the windows, are set in wooden frames. There are two entrances, both of which have inner and outer doors. The color scheme is a warm mocha brown; the base of the counter is tiled in ivory, black, and pink. We can't imagine who would come up with these diner colors, but we love them.

Mary and Nick showed us their kitchen, which, like the rest of the diner, is kept immaculate. The fluted stainless steel over the grill, with its sunrise pattern, shines. Two of the original diner artifacts that we enjoyed seeing in use were the open glass sugar bowls and the white porcelain Hamilton Beach malt machine that still functions perfectly after thirty years of use.

Although all food is prepared fresh, with a different selection of specials daily, the diner is most noted for its omelettes. We particularly liked the Swiss cheese and spinach omelette, which was made with fried onions. There's something called an "Ellie's Omelette." Named after a friend of the owners, who invented it, this omelette is made from Swiss cheese, bacon, and fried onions.

Most of the customers at Marybill's are regulars who have been coming here for years. Many of them grew up with Mary Kolkos, and many of them now bring their children around.

One of the regular customers, David Steinberg (no, not *that* David Steinberg), has been coming into the diner for over ten years. David's only in his mid-thirties, but he's known one of the waitresses since he was a kid. It's that type of place.

Nick and Mary love the diner life. Nick says it's harder than his old job but the money's good. Most of all, though, they love talking with their customers and the friendliness that's a big part of the work.

Marybill's is only a block away from the Long Island railroad station. It's also convenient to travelers who are on their way to or from Jones Beach.

*Marybill interior*

128  *Pioneer Diner* ========================================

*Monticello, New York*

=========================================================

With the Monticello Raceway a scant half-mile away, this is a good place to stop before betting all your money or, afterward, for a victory celebration. A stainless steel diner, the Pioneer has been serving Monticello for twenty-five years.

Old Route 17 used to be the gateway to the Catskills and at one time was dotted with diners, but all that has changed since the superhighway was built in the late 1950s. Now most of the diners that remain have been remodeled. The Pioneer is one of the last of the old guard.

Owned by Dave Buxbaum, the Pioneer is well maintained, kept very clean, and has undergone some minor alterations, like the fake Tiffany chandeliers.

Dave doesn't wax eloquent about the life of a dinerman. A realist about the future of the diner in this era of fast food and fancy-looking restaurants, he depends on the summer trade and the quality of his food for his business. He says he can always tell which customers are New Yorkers, because they invariably eat twice as much as the locals. We pressed him on this, but he couldn't come up with an explanation for this phenomenon.

The Pioneer offers one of the most complete selections of burgers we've seen anywhere. There is even a shrimp burger on the menu, but we didn't try it. There are different daily specials, as well as a full menu. The specials, served with potato, vegetable, salad, and rolls, were all reasonably priced. We noticed baked meat loaf, liver with onions or bacon, pot roast, and roast tom turkey, all of which are prepared as specials. Hot sandwiches, such as turkey, meatball, or ham, are also served with potato, vegetable, and salad. Fried seafood—shrimp, scallops, flounder, and the like—is also available. The chances are good that your fish will have been frozen rather than fresh.

There's a full breakfast menu. At one time, a lox and onion omelette was offered, but Dave said that he had to cut it out when the cost of smoked salmon became prohibitive. He does serve bagels.

The Pioneer is one of the few diners that has a complete soda fountain. Besides the usual sundaes and milk shakes, Dave makes a chocolate egg cream that rivals the famous Gem Spa's in New York City.

Dave said that customers occasionally come in and make strange demands. One day the United Parcel Service driver came in for breakfast and, instead of ordering, simply said, "Surprise me." So Dave cooked him two sunnyside eggs and served them one up and one down. It must have been pretty surprising.

## Empire Diner

*New York, New York*

The Empire is a diner in a tuxedo. Built as a diner in the 1920s, its wooden interior was covered with stainless steel and Formica in the 1950s; more recently, it was dressed up into a happening. It's a diner beyond diners. And it ain't cheap.

Once a riot of color, now it's black, white, and silver. The ceiling is painted black enamel and the counter tops and tabletops are black glass. The dining room, recently added, lacks the feel of a diner that the Empire has managed, on some levels, to maintain.

This diner does not serve standard diner fare, and the prices are much higher than standard diner fare too. We had Maryland chicken—breaded chicken in a cream sauce— served with sautéed zucchini and rice. The sauce was a bit on the heavy side, and we found the chicken to be just plain greasy, although nicely seasoned with tarragon and lemon. We also had fettuccine; the pasta was served *al dente*, and strips of prosciutto ham and green pepper were mixed in. It was the pasta of the day, and quite good, though at those prices nothing special. The lentil soup was delicious, seasoned in such a way that it left a soft, sweet aftertaste. We were served a salad of romaine lettuce with slices of red bell pepper and bean sprouts. The Empire offers two dressings: Forest Green and creamy Roquefort.

The people who work at the Empire are not your usual diner help, because most of them are out-of-work actors or artists of some sort. One waiter, who deftly juggled oranges behind the counter while we had a pleasant talk with one of the owners, was an actor and a musician; the baker is a painter who sometimes add ingredients to her delicious desserts just for the sake of their color—all of which adds to the sense of a chic "in" place.

There is only one menu, available twenty-four hours a day, so whether you come in at 3:00 P.M. or 3:00 A.M., the same dishes are being served. Chili is a favorite at the Empire and is served with a condiment tray that includes chopped onion and sour cream. The stuffed mushroom appetizer is also in great demand, and there is a wide variety of omelettes—such as peas in cream sauce, artichoke, and scallions and cream cheese. A chef's salad made with turkey, tuna, alfalfa sprouts, Swiss cheese, hard-boiled eggs, and cherry tomatoes is always available.

The dessert menu is truly sensational. For example, the mocha cream pie comes with a gingerbread crust filled with a terrific mocha cream and topped with whipped cream and powdered cocoa. We could taste the real coffee beans that are used in the filling. Also offered, and equally delicious, were chocolate cream pie with coconut and butternut topping, and Brownie All the Way (a brownie topped with ice cream, hot fudge, and real whipped cream). The rice pudding has rum-soaked raisins in it. There's a blueberry cake and a banana cake; the blueberry cake has cranberries added to give a fluorescent red glow to the blueberry blue base.

The area in which the diner is situated, Chelsea, consists mainly of brownstone houses, factories, and warehouses. To the extreme west side of this neighborhood, by the river, there are quite a few gay leather bars. It's not uncommon to go into the Empire some night and see a very straight-looking couple from Westchester sitting next to two male lovers all decked out in leathers. Because the restaurant still has the basic look of a diner, it maintains some of the intimacy that diners are known for. So all these diverse types of people start talking to one another and wind up having a good time.

No one is sure who built the Empire, but judging by the wall clock over the kitchen door, it might have come from the Fodero Dining Car Company. Somewhere beneath all that glitter and hype is a real diner. Tenth Avenue is a truckers' highway. The view out the windows is of a Gulf station, a run-down red-brick apartment, and a huge warehouse with an equally huge advertisement painted on its wall. This is urban diner territory. Eating there amid all the soft lights, weekend piano music, and beautiful people is a little like slumming. It may look like a real diner, but there's little of the warmth that you feel in a real diner. The stars and would-be stars come out to be seen here, and there's something about it that left us with an uncomfortable feeling.

# River Diner

*New York, New York*

If we wanted to give friends visiting the city a true New York experience, we'd take them to the River Diner. Perched atop a small hill, the diner has a view across the Hudson River to the New Jersey Palisades. This is an industrial area, full of warehouses and near the freight yards. There's a constant flow of trucks up the cobblestoned avenue.

Perhaps the most surprising thing about the River Diner is its owner, Charlie Christides. A pleasant middle-aged man who got his early restaurant training as a boy in Greece, Charlie is a master chef. Before he took over this fifty-year-old Kullman diner in 1973, he had worked as head chef in some of New York's finer restaurants. Today he caters mostly to a working-class clientele, and while he likes his customers, we got the feeling that he misses cooking fine French foods for those who are used to and appreciate such foods.

One of the first things we noticed when we walked into this clean and attractive diner was the multicolored hair of one of the waitresses. The people on both sides of the counter spoke with thick New York City accents, and among the waitresses, gum-chewing was *de rigueur*. Everyone was friendly, and one of the waitresses, Pat, wore a button that read "I am a very hardworking New Yorker." Pat asked us why we were writing a book about diners. We told her how much we like them and how sick we are—and we think others feel the same way—of the plastic environments of the modern fast-food restaurants. "Oh, I hate those fast-food places," she told us. "My mother takes my kid to McDonald's for lunch. I tell her not to."

There have been a few minor changes in the appearance of the inside of this diner, such as new tiles on the wall behind the counter, where the menus are posted, and new chandeliers. But the changes serve to make the River clean and comfortable and do nothing to alter the original feel. Charlie told us about a seventy-year-old man who had come back to the River Diner for the first time in fifty years. As he stepped through the entrance he stopped in amazement. "You know," he said, "I used to eat in this diner regularly—breakfast, lunch, dinner. That was over forty-five years ago. I haven't been back since, and the place looks so nice and clean, just like before."

The building is about twenty feet long. The booths and the stools are both upholstered in blue, and above each booth is a small wall lamp with a white shade.

The food served at the River Diner reflects the culinary expertise of its owner. Everything is fresh, interestingly seasoned, and head and shoulders above regular city diner fare. There are different specials daily, and all are reasonably priced at about $3.00. One special we tried was the Ziti à la Chef. When Charlie cooks his pasta he boils it in the broth that's left over from cooking the chicken. The reusing of ingredients in this fashion is the best way to ensure freshness and avoid waste; it is also a secret of good cooking and the sign of an inventive and knowledgeable chef. The plain ziti boiled in broth gives the dish its flavor base. The boiled pasta is then placed in a pan and sautéed with fresh prosciutto ham, real Italian tomato sauce, butter, fresh garlic, Parmesan cheese, and a Greek cheese called *kefalotiri*. The ham is in strips, and pieces of green pepper are mixed in. The ziti was served in a ceramic serving dish that kept it hot, and a separate bowl of grated Parmesan cheese was placed on the table with it. This dish was easily as good as any pasta that we've had downtown in the renowned restaurants of Little Italy.

Another special we tried was the Chicken Legs Oreganata, made from two pieces of baked chicken seasoned with butter, fresh garlic, and white wine and served with a Turkish-style rice pilaf called *agem*.

Fridays bring such fish dishes as seafood crepes, made with a crab-meat, baby-shrimp, and fillet-of-sole filling and served on a bed of rice covered with a white-wine cream sauce.

In addition to all the slightly exotic dishes, there are plenty of standard diner dishes, such as meat loaf or roast beef.

Since the River is open from 5:00 A.M. to 5:00 P.M. there is no real dinner trade. Breakfast is a big meal here, and the French toast is excellent.

All soups are homemade. The chicken noodle soup was quite good, full of chunks of fresh chicken. Other soups include Yankee bean, clam chowder, and a French-style split pea soup made with small pieces of fresh carrot and Virginia ham.

The River Diner serves mostly the people who work in the area. The customers we saw all knew Charlie and his wife, Mina, who works behind the counter. The talk was familiar and frequently very personal. The diner does get foreign tourists, though, and in the summertime tour buses will stop there and the passengers and driver will come in for lunch.

It seems a shame that such good cooking goes unnoticed in this authentic diner tucked away on the far West Side of Manhattan. There are plans to build a convention center in that part of town; maybe the huge complex will bring more people to the River Diner to share in the pleasurable eating experience we had there.

**Square Diner**

*New York, New York*

New York is a city in a constant state of change, and Lower Manhattan is no exception. The area we were in, known as Tribeca, is full of old factory lofts that are being converted into loft living space at an incredible rate and at incredible prices. What was once a barren factory district is now prime real estate.

The Square Diner sits in the midst of this neighborhood. Located south of Canal Street, it faces a small square formed by the merging of Varick Street and West Broadway. A Kullman diner, it's been sitting on the same spot since 1945 and looks only slightly the worse for wear. The building is not very long, but it tapers into a small alcove, the corner of which is a wall of glass brick, and this creates the illusion of greater length.

There's plenty of stainless steel inside, and the floor is a blue-and-brown-checked tile mosaic. The tabletops and counter tops are blue Formica, and the stools are upholstered in blue. There are broad, vertical green stripes on the stainless steel exterior, and the red letters of a neon beer sign glow in the window. Like many old diners, the heating system is limited to two small space heaters, and any warmth you feel is radiated from the grill.

The big attraction in terms of food here is the charcoal

broiler. Steaks, burgers, liver—whatever you want—can be charbroiled for that extra flavor.

There are three different specials daily, in addition to the regular menu: Beef goulash, Salisbury steak, and roast chicken were the specials on one night we were there. These platters came with potato, vegetable, and bread and butter and cost about $3.00.

John Siderakis, the young Greek owner, makes a lot of soup. He says he serves between three and four hundred bowls a day in the wintertime. Vegetable, split pea, chicken, beef barley, and lentil soups are all homemade and are served daily.

We had liver steak and flank steak. We also tried the chicken, which was served with a rich, brown giblet gravy. The flank steak was charbroiled and quite tender. The liver had been cooked with onions and was slightly rare, so it was very flavorful and not at all tough. The vegetables were canned and forgettable, although the home fries were quite good.

Because it's surrounded by factories, living lofts, and office space, and is two blocks from a police stable and a firehouse, the Square gets a variety of clientele. While we were there we saw artists, cops, and just plain working Joes. And we saw a lot of soup consumed.

While we were talking with John, a woman called over from the counter, "Tell them about Chester!" It seemed that she knew more about this Chester than John did, so we asked her to join us. She told us that she had been eating at the Square Diner for nine years and that she had raised her kid there, teaching him to walk by having him push his walker up and down along the counter. Chester was the old grillman who had worked at the Square for thirty years. The woman told us that he was a pleasant and warmhearted sort of guy, always a pleasure to deal with. After Chester retired, she claims, her young son would ask for him regularly.

This woman was a real diner fan, and ran off a litany of diner names: Courthouse, Blue Sky, Midway, Yellowbird— all Long Island City diners where she used to eat regularly. She talked about the Square, how it was once an all-night diner and how she feels that one of the big attractions of a diner is that a woman can eat there alone and not be bothered or feel uncomfortable. She also talked about what she called "the student union complex" (a neurosis overlooked by Freud), wherein people will do their paperwork in a diner, because it is a public place—holdover from the days when they'd write their college papers in the student union.

We had coffee and dessert too. The cakes and pies are all delivered by a commercial bakery, but the rice pudding is homemade. The pudding was fresh and good but nothing exceptional.

Some of the things we overheard in the Square: the squawk of two-way police radios, "I can only drink Coke through a straw so it doesn't touch my teeth," and the inevitable "To stay or to go?" A sound we kept expecting to hear was John Belushi going, "Cheeseburger, cheeseburger."

*North Syracuse, New York*

Syracuse has the look of a diner town, and we expected to find quite a few diners while we were there. Unfortunately, with the exception of Mario's, almost all that we found were too run-down to recommend.

Mario's is *the* place to have breakfast or lunch in Syracuse. Run by Mario Biasi, who emigrated here from Bari, Italy, as a teenager, it's a clean and airy stainless steel Silk City.

Mario takes the diner business seriously. His aim is to satisfy each customer. When he first bought the diner, it was open for dinner, but Mario found that he didn't have enough time to devote to each customer, so he cut down the hours.

The house specialty is frittata, which is a mixture of home fries, onion, ham, and broccoli cooked together in a pan with eggs. Frittata is a dish that has its origins in Italy; literally translated it means "all mixed together" or "a mess." Whatever the translation, we found it delightful eating.

Watching Mario prepare frittata is a pleasure; it's seeing an artist at work. His approach to the frying pan is deliberate, and it is with great delicacy and care, almost as if he were performing a ritual, that he adds and stirs the ingredients. His movements are sometimes short and jabbing, at other times deft and graceful, as he sculpts each layer to ensure even browning in the pan.

We found that a Syracuse dining tradition is broccoli and eggs. We asked Mario about this obsession with broccoli, and he was as baffled as we were. When he first opened the diner, broccoli was not on the menu. His customers became so vocal in their demands for the vegetable that there were soon three main dishes that used it.

Besides the frittata, other dishes offered include breaded chicken cutlets (made with an egg-and-cracker breading), fresh haddock, ziti with meatballs, and, in the summer months, antipasto. At lunchtime Mario's wife, Lucretia, helps with the cooking.

The inside of Mario's has undergone some drastic renovations but the diner feel is unmistakable. The booths have been removed and replaced with tables, the walls are white Formica, and a drop ceiling has been added. The old steam table is now used to hold the muffins and breads. The green mosaic floor looks original, and the yellow-tiled counter base, with its green border, appears to have come with the diner.

Mario's is located three miles from the New York State Thruway and a quarter mile off Route 81, on an ugly strip with one fast-food joint after another. Fortunately, however, it is shielded from those monstrosities because it is set in the middle of a huge parking lot behind a supermarket. Since it is in such an open space and was built with large square windows, Mario's gets lots of light—so much that green bamboo curtains must be drawn in the morning to keep out the blinding sunlight. This casts a pleasant green hue throughout the diner.

## Suburban Skyliner

*Polksville, New York*

Interstate 81 cuts through the lush rolling hills and valleys of New York State. From this highway the Suburban Skyliner is visible, a memorable sight because it is two diners joined together. The first diner that meets the eye is the swan song of the once-great Silk City company. One of the last Silk City diners built, it was given to Frank and Marie Tinelli because of their close relationship with the company and their impeccable credit rating.

Frank is a big, burly man who is rarely seen without a cigar. Marie, his wife, is his perfect foil with her bright eyes and salt-and-pepper hair. Both are superb storytellers and are a virtual gold mine when it comes to the history of diners.

At one time, Marie owned a diner in neighboring Cortland and Frank ran the Skyliner. But Marie was baking such good pies and cakes at her place that she was attracting Frank's customers; so they decided to join forces.

Frank became interested in the science of diner construction when he first started out in the business. He would visit the Silk City plant to watch every stage of the construction of his diner. He also worked with the Parker brothers, out of New Rochelle, who were responsible for the transporting and installation of more diners than anyone else.

The inside of the Suburban Skyliner is aqua Formica and stainless steel. The place is kept bright and clean, and you can tell that the Tinellis run a tight ship.

Frank, one of the finest counter raconteurs we've run across, discoursed eloquently on the types of patrons who frequent diners. He has kind feelings toward them all, with the exception of the dreaded WPA customer (water, piss, and air). These folks come in just to use the facilities, bother the counterman for a glass of water, and then proceed to take up space, something Frank can't abide. Frank also debated the popular myth that service is faster at the counter, especially since the grill has been moved to the back in the modern diner. He claims that if the service is right, it will take the same amount of time to be served in a booth as at the counter. Who were we to argue?

In addition to a full-sized menu, the Skyliner offers different daily specials. One such special is chicken and biscuits, which consists of chunks of chicken with gravy over soda biscuits. With potato and vegetable, this dish costs about $3.00. Chicken and biscuits is one of Marie's favorite recipes. She used to cook it for the farmhands when she lived on a farm.

Among the dinners is the Delmonico steak, ten ounces of choice beef, served with fried onion rings, for slightly over $6.00. Fried honey-dipped chicken, broiled pork chops, and a "Beef and Sea" (a small sirloin served with fried shrimp) are also regular features of the menu. Beer is served.

Frank and Marie are in a state of semi-retirement, and their son Peter helps run the diner. It has always been a family business, with their daughter and other son helping out. They talk about all the help as though they were family. The Tinellis view working in a diner as a character-building experience. They speak fondly of young workers, who they feel were able to come to grips with themselves through the experience of dealing with the diner public. The diner is obviously more than a business to the Tinellis; it's truly a way of life.

*Schenectady, New York*

Ruby's Silver Diner is the only diner we've come across that was actually a converted railroad car, but you'd never know it just to look at it. The domain of one Ruben Michelson, this mahogany-paneled beauty is the home of some of the best potato salad we ever had on the road.

Ruby has been in the restaurant business in Schenectady for over twenty-five years. Prior to owning this diner, he had Ruby's Luncheonette for eighteen years—before the city bought him out and tore down the luncheonette to make way for a parking lot. He then took over the Silver Diner, changed the name to Ruby's Silver Diner, and continued to serve the same high-quality food that's kept some of his customers coming back every day for years and years.

The building was converted from a railroad car by splitting the car down the middle lengthwise and then across the width, and spreading it all out. Ruby's not sure exactly who did this or when, but he knows it was over forty years ago. The walls are all mahogany, some of them with inlay, and the booths are made from the same rich, dark wood. The tabletops are green, as are the stools and the vent windows along the ceiling. The walls are also decorated with mirrors, and at the far end there are dairy-farm scenes from Pine Grove Farms—pictures of calves and fields and barns—provided by the people who supplied the milk.

There is lots of stainless steel behind the counter, and Ruby's has the only concave grill hood we've seen. The kitchen is down in the basement, so food and dishes and the like are sent upstairs by a water-powered dumbwaiter which was custom-built for the diner. Because of the way it was built, you can stand outside the diner, look at its red and black exterior from several angles, and never be quite sure how big the place really is.

Ruby, who presides over his establishment in restaurant whites, a soda-jerk hat, and bifocals, said that he enjoyed the repartee with his customers, most of whom work at the local General Electric plant. Winnie, one of the waitresses, agreed. "I'll tell you," she said, "if you ever sat around and watched this place, we got it all over Mel's Diner." She was referring to the TV show *Alice*, a situation comedy that takes place in a diner.

Soon a customer walked in whom Ruby referred to as "the Commander." We asked him why and were told that he was the commander of the local chapter of the Jewish War Veterans, to which Ruby belongs. The Commander gave us the "naval salute," where you salute from the navel. Then, when Ruby told him that we were writing a book, the Commander called out, "Tell them about the book you're writing, Ruby: *Sex After Death*, or *How to Get Laid in the Coffin*."

Ruby's Diner serves mostly breakfast and lunch and can feed five or six hundred people in one day in a diner that seats eighty. All food is fresh and very reasonably priced.

There are different specials every day. We tried the stuffed pepper with potato salad for $1.85. We got one green pepper, which was stuffed to the point of bursting with ground beef and covered with tomato sauce. The portion of potato salad was enormous and, as we said, as good as any we've had. The salad was made with lots of egg and mayonnaise, and the platter was served with two slices of fresh, bakery Jewish rye bread, the type we thought existed only in New York City. Other specials include meat loaf and a baked-shells-with-hamburger dish that Ruby says is like a goulash.

We noticed a fresh roasted ham steak, and Ruby told us that he does everything himself, including making his own corned beef. In addition to the potato salad, he makes a macaroni salad and fresh coleslaw. The soups, all made from scratch, include Yankee bean, vegetable, Manhattan and New England clam chowders, and chicken noodle, and there's chili daily. The fish fillet sandwich is made from fresh fish. For dessert, there are homemade puddings: rice, bread, and tapioca.

Ruby said, "I knew I'd be somewhere, someplace, sometime, but never in a book." Well, Ruby, here you are.

*West Taghkanic, New York*

We enjoyed our visit to this diner, but friends and relatives have come back with less-than-glowing reports about the food. We find this hard to believe, but it does temper what would otherwise be an enthusiastic recommendation. Try it yourself, and let us know how you liked it.

The West Taghkanic Diner is a shiny, stainless steel Mountain View diner, built in 1954, that sits just off the Taconic Parkway. A huge neon Indian head in full headdress makes it impossible to miss from the highway. Other diners along this roadway have the same neon sign, and at one time they were all owned by the same person, but this is no longer true. The West Taghkanic is a separate entity and has no connection with any other diner.

Run by the Diande family, this diner is a monument to cleanliness. The decor is blue and white enamel, with plenty of fluted stainless steel behind the counter. The booths and stools are blue, the counter top is white, and potted plants hang in the large picture windows. Joan Diande and her daughters have warmed this gleaming diner's decor with handmade Raggedy Ann dolls that are prominently displayed.

Joan does most of the cooking herself, and her Italian specialties are made just like she prepares them at home. We tried the mostaccioli with sausage and found it to be excellent

(mostaccioli is a large ribbed macaroni). The sausages were flavorful, and the tomato sauce was homemade.

The house specialty is minestrone soup, which is made from scratch and so thick with vegetables that there's hardly room for the broth. The applesauce is homemade too—a diner first for us. The Diandes do much of their own baking, and we recommend the pies.

The high prices at this diner are fixed for the tourist trade. There's a breakfast menu that lists several specials, but the selections are not cheap; pancakes and sausage will run you about $3.00. But the proximity to the parkway and the clean and pleasant surroundings make it a worthwhile place to stop.

Some of the other specials offered are stuffed peppers Italian-style, roast beef, roast Virginia ham, and meat loaf with tomato sauce. Homemade chili is always available; we found it nice and spicy without being too hot.

Beer is served at the West Taghkanic, but people are discouraged from coming in just to drink. Genesee is the local brand, but imported beers are available with your dinner.

There are plenty of sandwiches, and a complete soda fountain. Butter is used on all sandwiches unless otherwise requested.

We were suspicious of the ketchup. The label on the bottle said "Heinz," but it poured too fast for us to be sure.

The inside of this diner is gorgeous and very comfortable. Old jukeboxes are at each booth—the type where you turn the pages with the lever at the top to read the selections, then press the buttons on the side to hear your tune. And because the diner is in a somewhat wooded area, it's possible to see an occasional deer or pheasant while you're eating.

# Rhode Island

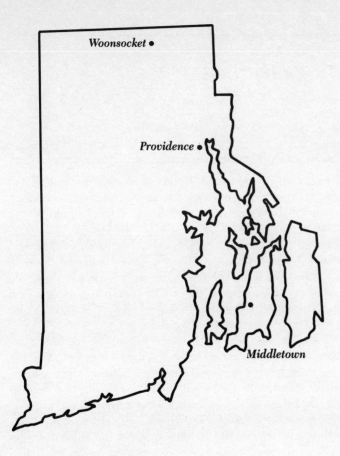

Woonsocket •

Providence •

Middletown

*Tommy's Deluxe interior*

## *Tommy's Deluxe Diner*

*Middletown, Rhode Island*

Middletown, Rhode Island, is close to Newport, the home of many a mansion. Tommy's Deluxe is a mansion among diners. An all-original 1941 O'Mahony, it stands impressively in a huge parking lot.

Demo, who runs it along with his two sisters, Chris and Sophie, loves his diner. The three of them are quite a trio—lively folks who enjoy working around people. Not only do they have a gorgeous diner, they serve top-quality food too. The stuffed chicken dinner we had was as good as any meal we were ever served in a diner.

When Tommy's was first brought to town, it was hauled in late at night on its own wheels with a police escort. This big event drew people from all over. The front axle and wheels are still intact, and the diner, even today, could be hooked up to the cab of a truck and taken away in one piece.

There are several striking touches inside this predominantly green diner. The slender bases of the stools have an octagonal shape, the counter top is made from green Italian marble, one of a kind, and the counter has a built-in glass showcase. You get a choice of cups for your coffee, either the standard cup and saucer or an earthenware mug. Two old jukeboxes, no longer functioning, add to the decor. The diner, which was purchased from Al Mack, the diner king of

Fall River, Massachusetts, is decorated with yellow and green tile along the wall next to the booths. There are two art-deco sunburst designs behind the counter, and early Formica on the ceiling. Outside, one of the impressive features of Tommy's Deluxe is the original steel clock that bears the diner's name.

The two sisters, Chris and Sophie, are quite a pair. Like a vaudeville team, they have all the answers before you even get a chance to ask the questions. They had a million stories, and they didn't just tell them, they acted each one out. Chris said that her most embarrassing moment was what she calls "the milk story." A customer came in and sat down at the counter. Chris asked, "What'll it be?" He ordered dinner with a glass of milk. She went to the window, brought it back, and proceeded to spill the milk in his lap. The next night the same customer returned. Again she asked him, "What'll it be?" He ordered the same thing, and she spilled the milk all over him in exactly the same way. The third day he came in again, took one look at her, and quickly said, "Just water, please."

The three siblings are all quite animated. Demo told us he once asked a customer what vegetable he wanted and walked away. The waitress came up to the same customer and asked him what vegetable he wanted. When another waitress asked him the same question a third time, the poor customer became so frustrated that he stood up and screamed, "Carrots and peas, carrots and peas, carrots and peas!" When Demo told the story, he mimicked the customer perfectly, shouting so loudly himself that the entire diner stopped to see what was going on.

Besides the stuffed chicken, which is a whole breast of chicken sautéed and served over stuffing with gravy, there is

*The steamtable*

142   a Portuguese soup, which is a meal in itself, made from spicy sausage, kale, beans, and potatoes. On some Fridays oyster stew, made to order and rich in cream and butter, is available. *Charissa*, a Portuguese sausage, is served as a sandwich with cooked tomatoes and onions, or in an omelette. Thursday is the traditional New England boiled dinner, corned beef and cabbage. The clam chowder is the New England variety, and it's chockful of huge clams.

Everything is made fresh: the mashed potatoes, the coleslaw, even the gravy. And the helpings on the three-portioned plates are large. This is one of those diners where our mouths start to water when we just think about it!

When we first told Chris and Sophie that we were writing this book and that they were going to be in it, they said, "Yeah, sure." We don't think they ever believed us, so please, when you stop by, tell them we sent you. They're on the night shift, so if you want to see them at work—and you should—you'll have to go then.

*Preparing for the lunchtime crowd*

## *Ever Ready Diner*

*Providence, Rhode Island*

We had heard, from longtime dinermen, what diners used to be like in the 1920s and 1930s. A visit to the Ever Ready is a trip into the diners of the past, when the lunch wagon was a man's domain and a woman was never seen. At least we never saw a woman inside when we were there, and it's hard to imagine one sitting at the counter.

The Ever Ready is a 1920s Worcester Lunch Car that has changed little over the years. Built in the era before there were any booths, the building is quite small and narrow. Inside, it's mostly white tile, with a green mosaic pattern at the base of the counter and along the walls beneath the windows. The white barreled ceiling has a band of red running down the middle. The kitchen is in the basement, and there are two grills, a small stove, and a steam table behind the marble counter. Some of the warmers used for holding food in the steam table are the original procelain ones. These are rare to see; they're no longer manufactured, and most of the old warmers are long since broken.

When we first arrived at the diner, we asked to see Roger, one of the owners whom we had spoken to on the phone. We were told to go around back and down to the basement. Once we found Roger—working in the kitchen down there—he told us that he hadn't been upstairs for fifteen years, that the kitchen was where he spent all his working hours. Roger loves the diner world, and he speculated on the future of the Ever Ready, which he felt was rather dim. None of his or his partner's children have any interest in taking over the diner, and he feels that when he goes the diner will go too.

The Ever Ready started life as a dog wagon, and hot dogs are still a big part of the menu. One of the two grills is used mainly for the toasting of frankfurter buns. The dogs themselves are boiled. A hot dog with everything on it, or "all the way," is called a "Sinatra." "All the way" includes mustard, relish, celery salt, and onion. A Sinatra for breakfast is a truly unforgettable experience.

Baked beans with eggs for breakfast is the norm at the Ever Ready. Two eggs—with beans, ham, toast, and coffee—cost a little more than $2.00. The franks cost about 55 cents. Besides the beef stew, which is always available, there is a different special every day. The specials cost about $2.00, and the menu runs like this: Monday, baked meat loaf; Tuesday, baked sausage; Wednesday, roast turkey or pot roast; Thursday, corned beef and cabbage; Friday, fish cakes with baked beans and fish-and-chips. This schedule never varies.

As we said, the Ever Ready is the domain of the working man. It is not a family diner or a place to take a date. Governors, judges, mayors, and local businessmen are known to lunch at this institution. It's like a clubhouse for grown-up kids. We found everyone there to be friendly, and the atmosphere is certainly relaxed. Check it out for yourself. It's a part of the diner experience, and one that you're not likely to forget.

*Haven Brothers, a modern-day night owl*

## Haven Brothers

*Providence, Rhode Island*

*"Mustard, Mac?"*

According to diner lore, Providence, Rhode Island, became the home of the first diner when a man named Walter Scott, back in 1872, hitched his horse to a wagon filled with pies, coffee, and sandwiches and then hauled it around town, selling from a different downtown location every night. Haven Brothers is a direct descendant of Walter Scott's "night owl." Set on the back of a truck, it's hauled behind city hall every evening at 5:00 and serves food there until 2:45 each morning. This has been going on for 110 years. The diner gets its power by hooking up to the streetlight outside city hall.

We visited Haven Brothers at two different times—8:00 P.M. and 2:00 A.M.—and it was jammed with customers at both hours. Inside the diner, which is all steel, there are narrow counters with stools that run along three of the walls. There's only room enough for eight stools, and many customers eat standing up. All food is prepared at the end of the diner, where there's a small grill and steam table. The fellow behind the counter was like a conveyor belt, handing out lobster rolls, beef stew, and cups of coffee. He addresses all his customers as "Mac." If you order a dog, he'll ask you, "How do you take it, Mac?" or, "Mustard, Mac?"

There's a small plaque inside the diner saying that a Greg Morse was the builder. No one seemed to know much about him, or maybe they're just tired of answering questions about the place—they must get asked a million. We did hear, from

*Our friends at Haven Brothers.*

several people, that the diner is a hundred years old and used to be horse-drawn. Standing inside this modern-day "Night Owl," it seemed more than possible.

The menu is very simple. Lobster roll appeared to be the best-selling item, and it was delicious. We ate several, at about $2.50 each. Piping-hot beef stew is another staple here, served in a soup bowl for 75 cents. There was plenty of meat and huge chunks of potato, even if the broth was kind of thin. A bowl of kidney bean soup was offered for about the same price as the stew, and we saw plenty of hot dogs and coffee consumed. In addition to all the people eating inside, there's a takeout window located at the back of the diner.

We saw what looked like a shopping-bag lady hanging around outside the diner, but we soon realized she was one of the workers. Every fifteen minutes she'd clear all the used paper plates and napkins out of the diner, keeping the place clean. We understand that Senator Beard once took her to Washington as his guest.

Later on, we discovered that we had foolishly locked ourselves out of our car, with the keys still inside (it was late, and we'd been driving all day). We asked everyone in the diner if they had a wire coat hanger we could use to break into the car, but all we got were stony stares. Finally we asked our bag-lady friend. Without saying a word, she walked over to a large plastic bag in the cab of a truck, reached inside without looking, and, almost as if by magic, pulled out the necessary tool. Her effortlessness made it seem as though it were an apparition. Just another of those small occurrences that kept cropping up to amaze us on the diner trail.

You might want to visit another, similar wagon, called Mike's, parked outside Union Station in Providence. If you do, let us know how you think they compare.

## Silver Top Diner

*Providence, Rhode Island*

Because of the strange hours, the scene at the Silver Top Diner is more unusual than the scene at most other diners. It opens at midnight and closes at ten in the morning. Almost everything else in Providence, including the bars, closes at 1:00 A.M., so there aren't too many other places to go. The Silver Top caters to the after-bar crowd, the many college students in town, and those people who work until late at night and are looking for someplace to eat. Once inside the diner, the party starts. Everyone's having a good time, and the feeling is contagious.

The Silver Top is a 1941 Kullman diner, and it's a beauty both inside and out. A huge sign on the roof spells out the name in silver and red letters against a blue background. There are blue-enameled vertical stripes decorating the stainless steel walls; two front doors, side by side, sheltered by a blue and white metal awning; and lots of glass brick. There used to be two blue-glass windows next to the entrance, but they had to be boarded over after an attack by vandals. Signs bordering the streamlined monitor roof advertise infrared broiling, air conditioning, and vaculator coffee.

Inside, there are powder-blue tiles along the base of the counter and light-blue tiles on the floor, and an ivory-colored grill hood with art-deco chevrons inlaid for design. The wooden booths are high-backed, and the white ceiling is grained with a blue marble pattern. The diner is all original, but it does show some signs of the wear and tear of almost forty years of use.

Another unusual feature of the Silver Top is that there are no daily specials. As a matter of fact, no full dinners of any kind are served at this diner. It's mostly eggs, omelettes, burgers, and homemade baked goods, which are excellent. We spoke with Lisa, the owner's attractive young daughter, who told us that her dad learned to bake from an elderly baker friend of his, now retired. Breakfast muffins are a big thing at this diner, and we mean that in more ways than one. Not only are they very popular, but they're enormous. We tried the blueberry muffins, hot and buttered, with a good cup of coffee—almost a meal in itself. Other baked goods include cinnamon Danish and apple turnovers, both of which are of high quality.

At the Silver Top you can have any type of omelette you want, and we mean any type—you name it and they'll cook it. The burger selection is also extensive. Our favorite is the mushroom burger, cooked in butter right on the grill, with fresh mushrooms.

For breakfast we recommend the French toast, made with vanilla extract; it costs about $1.00. Blueberry pancakes are not on the menu but are available if you request them. The pancakes are priced slightly higher than the French toast. Two eggs with coffee will also run you about $1.00. Eggs with bacon, home fries, and coffee will cost over $2.00.

The Silver Top attracts quite a cross section of clientele. We met Eddie, a garrulous ex-cabbie who comes in every night. Eddie looks so much like a retired cabbie that he might have been sent over by Central Casting. It's easy to see that he's perfected the art of small talk through his years behind the wheel. And Lisa told us about Annie, the placid, Zenlike grillmaster, who's now retired. We also heard about a group of students from the Rhode Island School of Design who came in one night dressed in their pajamas. We looked at the students around us, many of whom sported long hair and beads and appeared to be slightly intoxicated, and felt a sense of 1960s *deja vu*. Had we slipped through a time warp? Anything seemed possible in the Silver Top at 3:00 A.M.

The Silver Top, situated in an industrial part of town, is easy to get to but hard to find because it's set back from the road and nothing else around is open. Look carefully as you drive down the street; you won't want to miss it.

## Champ's Diner

*Woonsocket, Rhode Island*

At lunchtime, customers stand inside Champ's Diner, waiting for one of the fourteen stools to become empty so they can sit down to a good, quick meal served over a marble counter. Barrel-roofed, box-shaped, and painted bright red, this 1926 Worcester Lunch Car is reminiscent of an old trolley. It's been in the Champaigne family since 1935, when Ovila Champaigne bought it. It's now run by his sons, Roger P. and Gerry, who have been working there for over forty years.

Like many old diners that were built before the invention of the booth, Champ's is a man's diner. Conversation turns mainly to sports, and Red Sox scores are important, although Roger follows the Tigers—and believe it or not, there are some Yankees fans up there. Woonsocket is a big hockey town too. As a matter of fact, Roger, who's sixty years old and looks trim and fit in his whites and soda-jerk hat, was going home at 2:00 P.M., after having been to work at 4:00 A.M., in order to rest up for a hockey game that night. He was going not as a spectator but as the oldest player in an "over-thirty" hockey league. That's how he relaxes and unwinds after a hard day behind the counter.

Although the diner serves mainly men, women are always welcome. As a matter of fact, you could almost mistake Champ's for a Bible-belt diner, because Roger insists that no

*Champ's Diner*

foul language be spoken on the premises. The local paper had a picture of one of the townswomen sipping coffee at the counter. The caption read: "Stopping off at Champ's for a cup of coffee is a local tradition."

The menus at Champ's are handwritten in crayons of different colors and decorated with corny cartoons cut from 1950s-style magazines. The food selections are fairly simple, and they're all fresh. We had chicken croquettes, which were oblong in shape and fried golden brown. The chicken had been ground fine, which made for a very smooth taste. The meal was served on a three-portioned plate, and the platter included fresh carrots, real mashed potatoes with gravy, and salad. Also on the menu is American chop suey, a New England specialty. This is pasta shells mixed with ground meat and tomato sauce; the sauce was flavorful, but the shells were overdone.

There are no home fries at this diner, and we asked Roger why. "We never had 'em," he said. "A lot of people ask for them, but we never had 'em." Customers have baked beans with breakfast. Champ's makes them with sugar, salt, pepper, onion, molasses, and of course beans. They cook for three or four hours before they're ready to be served.

All the muffins and puddings at the Champaignes' diner are made in the kitchen. In addition to the usual blueberry, corn, and bran, the brothers bake strawberry muffins once a week.

One special a day is featured. For instance, Friday it's fresh fish, haddock, or cod, fried or baked. Wednesday it's meat loaf, and Thursday it's boiled dinner, corned beef and cabbage. The soup selections, which include tomato, chicken, and clam chowder, are all homemade. Steamed dogs, roast beef, and pork sausage are always available, and on Fridays there's lobster roll. Everything in the place is served for about $3.00 or less.

Roger told us that he looks upon the diner as the original fast-food service, and his movements behind the counter prove it. At lunchtime he's faster than a speeding bullet. Able to leap tall buildings in a single bound? No, but if he's as fast on the ice as he is at the grill, he's got to be a great hockey player.

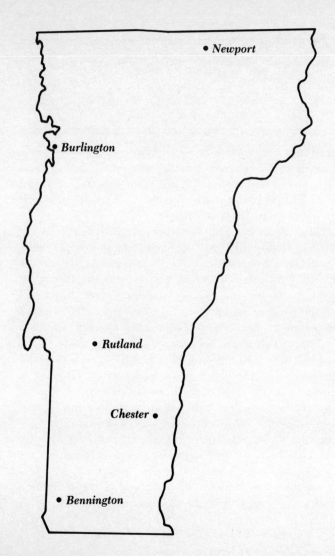

# Vermont

• Newport

• Burlington

• Rutland

Chester •

• Bennington

*The Blue Benn Diner*

## Blue Benn Diner

*Bennington, Vermont*

If you're into health foods or vegeterian cooking, you'll love the Blue Benn Diner. Even if you're not, you'll probably still love the place; everyone we spoke to in Bennington raved about it. The people in the next booth told us that the food was great before we even ordered.

The Blue Benn is a Silk City diner, most likely from the late 1940s or early 1950s. Outside, it's stainless steel decorated with yellow enamel and blue piping. Inside, there's the classic Silk City barreled ceiling that creates the illusion of being in a railroad car, lots of stainless steel, and wood around the window frames.

Bennington is the home of Bennington College, so you'll see a mixture of students and townspeople at the diner.

Sonny Monroe, owner of the Blue Benn, is a local boy who got turned on to natural foods while working in the kitchen of another restaurant. The cook there had a subscription to *Prevention* magazine, a publication that preaches health through proper diet. After the cook quit, his magazines kept coming, and Sonny started reading them. He liked what he read and has been a vegetarian ever since. Because of this, Sonny offers at least one vegetarian dish daily.

Among the more unusual items served is the *tabouli*, a sandwich made from bulgur, tomato, bean sprouts, and parsley on pita bread. There is also a full selection of herbal teas, and honey is available as a sweetener. For cereal, three types of granola are available; apple bran, raisin bran, and sunflower crunch.

Omelettes are a big item at this diner. There's ham and cheese, Vermont cheddar cheese, watercress and cream cheese, fresh mushroom, and the Blue Benn special omelette, which is made with ratatouille. Three types of pancakes are listed on the menu; plain, blueberry, and buckwheat. Real maple syrup is available, as are bagels and cream cheese.

Regular dinners include fried haddock, fried whole clams, chicken and dumplings, link sausage on mashed potatoes, roast turkey, roast beef, and half a fried chicken with cranberry sauce. All dinners are reasonably priced at about $3.00 and come with potato, vegetable, and rolls and butter. The Blue Benn is one of those rare diners that makes its own mashed potatoes and its own french fries.

Perhaps the highlight of this diner is the baked goods. Muffins are homemade (blueberry, corn, bran), and Sonny's mother-in-law bakes carrot cake and zucchini bread whenever she's in the mood. Fortunately, she had been in the mood just before we got there, because the carrot cake was excellent. The cheesecake is of high quality, and if you're lucky enough to get there in season, you must try the rhubarb pie—the only true rhubarb pie we found on the road. Made from fresh rhubarb, no strawberry filler added, and with a light crust, it's out of this world.

There's a sign outside the diner that is supposed to depict someone enjoying a cup of coffee and licking his lips. Instead, it looks like he's choking. Don't be deceived. The Blue Benn serves a hearty cup of coffee. Try a cup, along with one of the fresh buttermilk donuts.

Be sure to sign the guest book while you're there. Francine Lipschitz of Walla Walla, Washington, did. Her comments read that this is the best food in Bennington. Many of the signers gave the diner four stars. We do too.

*South Burlington, Vermont*

We'll always have a soft spot in our hearts for the Parkway Diner. While we were in that part of the world, word got out to one of the local TV stations that two lone diner hunters were visiting some of the better-known local eateries, the ones people just kind of took for granted. We were met at the Parkway by a reporter and camera crew who filmed us for the local news. They let us talk about our love for the lunch car and why we feel that it's important for people to recognize these establishments' worth. Folks up there have a real fondness for their diners, and considering all the good home cooking that goes on in them, that's no surprise.

We were hosted by the owners' dark-haired son, Peter Hatgen, who is young, handsome, and personable. For some reason Peter would wink at us whenever he thought that he had made a particularly salient point about diner life. We wrote this off to the fact that he was a high school student trying to impart wisdom.

Most of the customers at the Parkway are regulars, and they are all treated well. As Peter said, "You go out of the way for your steady customers." But don't worry, they treat strangers fine, too. A lot of Canadians stop by the Parkway on their trips south, and it's also a favorite with truck drivers. We asked Peter how truckers find diners, and he told us it's mostly through talks with other truckers on their CB radios.

Prices are quite reasonable at the Parkway, and the food is good. Breakfast is a big meal here, and the breakfast specials all feature a cold cereal in addition to your eggs: Mostly it's Kellogg's Special K or corn flakes, Rice Krispies, or bran flakes. We weren't there for breakfast, and when we looked at the menu we didn't notice any mention of home fries, so you should ask about potatoes if you want them. They do serve pancakes, French toast, donuts, English muffins, and cinnamon toast.

All soups are homemade, and besides the chowder, bean, and chicken soups they make a Greek-style lemon soup that is very good.

Most dinners are served for about $3.00. The most expensive item we saw offered was a tenderloin steak sandwich which, with french fries and coleslaw, cost around $4.75. The Southern fried chicken, with bread and butter, potato and vegetable, costs less than $3.00.

There are plenty of sandwiches on the menu, and a roast beef special, served on pumpernickel roll, with french fries, was being offered for just over $2.00. We also tried the lobster salad roll, which is a commercial salad, and loved it. The chicken salad, which is fresh, is also recommended.

For dessert the owners make their own bread pudding, which has orange peel and raisins for extra flavoring.

Not only is Schlitz and Molson beer available on tap, and Budweiser in bottles, but a white burgundy and a red wine are also offered. This could be because the owners are Greek, and there's a slight sense of the European here.

Peter's cousin was behind the counter with him that day. Her family had once owned the Bellows Falls diner, which we never had a chance to visit. So if you're in that part of Vermont, check out the Miss Bellows Falls and let us know if we've missed anything.

## Delaney's Country Girl Diner

*Chester, Vermont*

If you're looking for a "get away from it all" weekend, we recommend Chester, Vermont. You could stay in this charming New England town and take your meals at Delaney's Country Girl Diner.

Delaney's Country Girl is a family business, run by Mike and Carole Delaney with lots of help from their teenage daughter. All food served is made from scratch, and the corn and tomato chowder is renowned.

The Delaneys moved to Chester from Connecticut over ten years ago and took over this diner. There has been a diner at the location for forty years, but not always a shiny, stainless steel lunch car. The previous structure was a little red Worcester Lunch Car, and many of the townspeople found that easier to relate to than the current model, which is too "citified" for their tastes. Some of these Green Mountain Yankees have a definite resistance to change and can be very clannish. They refer to anyone who comes from as far south as Massachusetts as a "flatlander." To some of these old-timers, a flatlander is a slightly lower form of life. Nevertheless, there's a true mix of locals and flatlanders eating at the Country Girl these days, a testimony to the Delaneys' independent spirit as well as to the superior quality of their cooking.

Chester is in the heart of ski country, and in the wintertime the place is full of skiers looking for a good solid breakfast. Pancakes and sausage is a favorite. The pancake

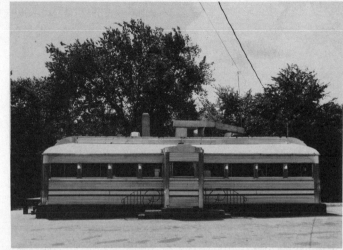

*Delaney's Country Girl Diner*

*Mike Delaney*

156 batter is made from scratch, not a mix. Carole says it's just like her father used to make. The sausages are a local product, supplied by the Jameson Market right in town; they're all pork, slightly spicy, and available at breakfast time only. There is real Vermont maple syrup for your pancakes; the diner serves as an outlet for a local sugarer, and you can buy a bottle to take home. The Delaney's make a delicious blueberry muffin. Order a basketful—that's how they come.

The specialty of the house is corn and tomato chowder. Made from butter, onion, corn, tomato, egg yolks, heavy cream, a little sugar, bay leaf, and other seasonings, it's worth the trip. Reasonably priced at 45 cents a cup and 60 cents a bowl, the chowder is always available.

Also homemade are the potato salad, coleslaw, pies, and puddings. Indian and bread pudding are available. On the menu is written: "For better or worse, our food is prepared in our own kitchen."

The menu is not extensive, but there is a good selection. Several types of sandwiches are offered, including a Reuben which is made from grilled pastrami, sauerkraut, and Swiss cheese. The grilled cheese sandwich is made with tangy Vermont cheddar, as is the grilled ham and cheese sandwich; you can have the cheddar on your cheeseburger too. For those of you who like something different in burgers, try a Chesterburger, which is a hamburger with bacon, cheese, lettuce, tomato, and mayonnaise for about $2.00.

The most expensive item is the roast beef dinner, which goes for about $4.00. Other specials include fillet of haddock (fresh fish dipped in the Delaneys' own batter), baked ham, breaded veal patty, honeycomb pickled tripe, and of course meat loaf. Dinner comes with a choice of two vegetables, and homemade bread and rolls.

One attraction of visiting diners is the people that you meet on both sides of the counter. We saw a fellow at the Country Girl who took us by surprise. He was a trim and fit octogenarian horse trainer who spoke with a British accent and was impeccably dressed in brown knee socks and penny loafers, tan Levi shorts, and an old but freshly laundered long-sleeve shirt with button-down collar. His mustache was well-trimmed and his hair close-cut, and he had a healthy tan. Sitting at the counter, he talked horses while smoking a cigarette. He was talking about the young jockey Steve Cauthen, who had just moved to England after experiencing a run of bad luck. What made Cauthen such a great jockey, he said, were his hands. His touch communicates something to the horses that makes it want to respond.

When you visit Delaney's Country Girl Diner, be sure to look at the clock; it runs on Vermont Standard Time year-round.

## Miss Newport Diner

*Newport, Vermont*

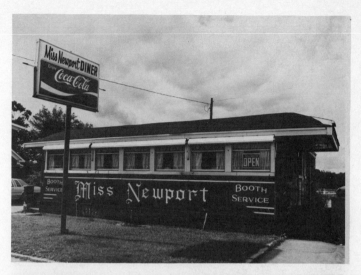

The part of northern Vermont where the Miss Newport Diner is located is called the Northeast Kingdom, and once you see it you'll know why. The huge mountains have such a sense of power and majesty that you feel like you're in a mythical kingdom—and the Miss Newport is beautiful enough to be the crown jewel.

The Miss Newport is a bright-red enamel Worcester Lunch Car, built in 1944 and so well maintained that it could be a diner museum. Its barreled roof is pink, the marble counter top is a light brown, and there's mocha-colored porcelain with red trim behind the counter. The original floor, tiled in a blue and brown checkerboard mosaic, has stood the test of time and still looks brand-new. The wooden booths are red and blue, and the stools are upholstered in red. There's lots of wood inside, and red-checked curtains at the windows. The whole place feels very homey.

The current owner, Fred Etheze, who's had the diner for twelve years, told us how it was brought up from Worcester on a flatbed truck. It was such a wide load that they needed special permits to haul it through three states, and it had a police escort all the way.

Fred, who keeps his diner quite clean and shiny, says that most of his customers are regulars and that he knows what to put up as soon as he sees them walking through the door. But

*Midafternoon at the Miss Newport Diner*

he does get a fair number of tourists and vacationers, many of whom make a point of stopping at the Miss Newport every year as a part of their vacation. One such vactioner was Susan Belling, and we're grateful to her for introducing us to the Miss Newport.

Like most country diners, all food served here is fresh. Fred says he hates to use anything canned. He opens for business at 5:00 A.M., but he's in the kitchen an hour and a half earlier every morning, preparing fresh roasts and baking muffins and pies.

Different specials are offered daily and are very reasonably priced. The average cost for a platter is $2.75, and that includes an entrée, potato, vegetable, tea or coffee, and homemade pudding. Popular dishes are the pot roast, the meat loaf, and the roast pork. Fred also makes beef stew, hot chicken sandwiches from a whole chicken, American chop suey, and fried haddock.

There's a full selection of sandwiches, most of which are priced under $1.00. Fred makes something called a "Freddy Burger," which is two patties that are put on the grill with cheese between them and onion on top and served on a bun with lettuce and tomato. You get six ounces of meat, and it's priced just over $1.00.

Soups are all homemade. On Fridays you'll find fish or corn chowder available. Fred makes vegetable beef soup and cabbage soup, as well as something called "Etheze Soup," made with hamburger meat, elbow macaroni, crushed tomato, onion, oregano, salt, and pepper. This has to be the most popular soup in town.

Fred also makes his own breakfast muffins and dessert pies. The muffin offerings consist of blueberry, apple, cranberry, corn, and raisin bran muffins. Of course, they are not all available on any given day. The pies are apple, pumpkin, blueberry, and an occasional chocolate cream. When it comes to pie fillings, Fred breaks his rule about no canned goods.

This part of Vermont is dairy country, and there's plenty of fresh milk. Chocolate pudding made from scratch with whole milk is available daily.

Breakfast is a big meal at the Miss Newport, and there is a large selection of omelettes. One is jokingly referred to as "the heartburn special," an onion, cheese, and tomato omelette. Served with home fries, toast, and coffee, it goes for about $1.25.

Fred moved to Newport from Portland, Maine, in the mid-1960s. He had been a truck dispatcher in Portland and was looking for a change. Since he had done some cooking in the army, when he heard about this diner being for sale he took a chance. Things paid off for him. He loves it up there in the country, and he loves serving his customers. He says he's always aware of the beauty of the Northeast Kingdom; he appreciates never having to rush and the peace and quiet that exists up there. This feeling is incorporated with the running of his diner, right down to small details like how he grinds his own coffee beans for that extra-fresh flavor.

If you go up to ski Jay Peak or to see the fall foliage or just to take a drive, we recommend stopping by Fred's. It's part of the experience.

## Midway Diner

*Rutland, Vermont*

The Midway Diner is the kind of place where the waitress will ask you, "What'll you have, fellas?" if you happen to be fellas. A 1951 Silk City diner, the Midway is set well off the road and is surrounded by a huge parking lot. The exterior is all stainless steel and is decorated with a brown and white awning. A horizontal white-enamel stripe on the outside of the diner is bordered with green and contains the diner's name in green lettering.

Nancy, a slender woman with dark-brown eyes, has been presiding over the dining area ever since the diner was brought into Rutland. She started working as a waitress part-time while still in high school. Most of the customers at the Midway are regulars, and Nancy knows them all. It's this sense of friendly familiarity that makes Nancy enjoy her job. And she looks after her customers. For example, if Charlie Davison, who lives alone and recently underwent open-heart surgery, doesn't show up for his usual meal, someone from the diner will check up on him to make sure he's okay.

We asked Nancy if she ever takes on the role of bartender and gives advice on personal problems. She replied that she'd rather not upset anyone's stomach while they're eating. We did see her take care of one customer, who complained about being allergic to the fat on his roast beef. Nancy gracefully obliged him by trimming every piece of fat off what appeared to be an already lean cut of beef.

The Midway is a twenty-four-hour diner and is open seven days a week. The menu is fairly extensive, and most of the food served is fresh. In the summer months all vegetables, such as squash, green beans, and native corn, are fresh-picked; in the winter they're canned or frozen.

We tried one special—the turkey shortcake—and found it filling and hearty. This is sliced turkey served over a soda biscuit and covered with gravy. A popular New England dish, the turkey came with potato and vegetable—all for only $2.00. Most of the fish served is fresh frozen. Baked stuffed clams are offered on the menu, a diner rarity. Chili is a regular feature, as are the beef stew and the oyster stew. A clam roll (fried clams on a hot-dog bun) is served with french fries and coleslaw for under $2.00.

There are several small touches that we appreciated at the Midway. For example, coffee beans are ground on the premises. And coffee is served in white china cups with a green stripe around the middle; cream comes in a matching china creamer. If you're a hunter or on a long drive or just like lots of coffee, you can get your caffeine fix to go by the pint or by the quart if you have your own thermos.

One of our favorite sandwiches, peanut butter and bacon, is served. Peanut butter is big at the Midway. A small paper cup full of peanut butter, the type that might contain jelly for toast, is available with your bread.

Real Vermont maple syrup for pancakes or French toast is sold in an unusual fashion. For 60 cents you can get a small bottle of syrup; the bottle looks just like the ones the airlines use to serve liquor.

A sign on the menu board behind the counter reads NO PETS OR RADIOS ALLOWED. Outside the diner, up by the roadway, is a tremendous sign alerting all who pass by that the Midway Diner and Restaurant is open twenty-four hours. You can't miss it.

Note: *These phrases were collected on the road during our research trips. Everything below was communicated to us verbally, usually by owner, employee, or customer. Some of these expressions are probably regional and are marked with an asterisk.*

*Adam and Eve on a raft:* poached eggs on toast

*Adam and Eve on a raft and wreck 'em:* same as above but with the yolks broken

*\*chelsea steak:* toast (Boston area)

*chocolate cow:* chocolate milk

*cow:* milk

*draw one:* one coffee

*dress 'em up:* an order to go

*drop two:* two poached eggs

*\*eighty-seven:* good-looking girl in booth (Maine)

*eighty-six:* cancel order or throw customer out

*fish eyes in glue:* tapioca

*fried cake:* donut

*graveyard stew:* milk toast

*java* or *joe:* coffee

*\*juke box:* microwave oven (New Jersey)

*popeye:* spinach

*slapjacks:* pancakes

*\*steam-heated room:* whorehouse (Portland, Maine)

*trilby:* an order topped with chopped onions (an old term rarely used today)

*\*truckburger:* cheeseburger with fried egg (eastern Massachusetts)

*two back:* two orders of the same thing

*two lookin' at ya:* two sunnyside eggs

*two to trot* or *put wings on two:* two coffees to go

*\*WPA customer:* stands for water, piss, and air, or a patron who spends no money (central New York)